PRAISE FOR DUN
MCPHERSON

Sojourn the Inner Heaven

"What a wonderful book! Poetic, personal, tender, imaginative, insightful, and mindful. It describes a process, explores it, and then, masterfully, explains how it can be accessed. Dunya guides our deeper understanding and gives us a road map for embodied enlightenment and spiritual bliss. No matter how much you already know, you will learn more in this book."
—Elisa de la Roche, Ph.D., actor, writer, artist, educator

"Poetic descriptions, effortless practices, and generous invitations expand the definition of meditation, serving to free the mind of *doing* so that one's breathing, moving body awakens in the great mystery of being alive...Guidance from a true master, one who reveres in every cell of her body the precious dance of all living beings."
—Mary Abrams, MA, RSME, Founder of Moving Body Resources (NYC) & International Teacher

"As I started to read I felt the expansion of awareness that I feel when arriving and settling in a Dancemeditation session. Dunya has articulated the magic and merger of body mind spirit that is so big and palpable and mostly out of reach. This is beautiful!"
—Celeste Yacoboni, curatorial editor of *How Do You Pray*, Minister of The Walking Way

Skin of Glass

"...profound ideas, expressed in startlingly evocative language."
—Roger Copeland, author of *Merce Cunningham: The Modernizing of Modern Dance*

"Dreamy, deeply searching, and so smart kinesthetically...She journeys

through organs, bones, muscles, delving into an other realm of thinking. A wondrous and thought-provoking excursion."
— Janet Mansfield Soares, Professor of Dance Emerita, Barnard College, Columbia University

"McPherson succeeds in the almost impossible task she sets for herself: putting into words what is wholly nonverbal dance, and describing what is utterly indescribable mystical experience."
—Ruth Vincent, author of *Elixir* and *Unveiled*, Changeling P.I. novels

"Memoir, prose poem, erotic journey, mystical discourse and cultural commentary Dunya's brave book also launches a new genre of writing from the body. It is a book sorely needed by a culture disembodied..."
— Mary Bond, MA, author of *Your Body Mandala, Balancing Your Body*, & *The New Rules of Posture*

"She offers insights and inspiration on every page."
—Christopher Pilafian, Lecturer, Department of Theater & Dance, University of California, Santa Barbara

"A mystical page-turner! I read 'Skin of Glass' in two days all the way through, wishing, as I read, that there was a way I could inhale this book..."
—Jenna Woods, author of *The Dancing Cymbalist*

SOJOURN THE INNER HEAVEN

MOVEMENT MEDITATIONS FOR AWAKENING

DUNYA DIANNE MCPHERSON

DERVISH SOCIETY OF AMERICA

Dervish Society of America Edition, 2021

Sojourn the Inner Heaven: Movement Meditations for Awakening

Ebook ISBN: 978-0-9801986-3-8

Print book ISBN: 978-0-9801986-2-1

Cover photo: Daniel Falgerho

Author portrait: Paul B. Goode

For those who seek.

CONTENTS

SECTION TWO: TIME & FORCES
Dancemeditations for Knowing

SECTION THREE: DREAMING IN THE FLESH
Dancemeditations for Excavation & Exploration

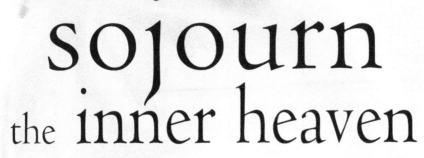

sojourn
the inner heaven
Movement Meditations for Awakening

dunya dianne mcpherson

Everybody has an 'Antarctic'—the place a person seeks to find answers about themselves.
—Thomas Pynchon

This is why we practice meditation—
so that we can treat ourselves more compassionately...
live lives of greater connection; and, even in the face of challenges,
stay in touch with what we really care about.
—Sharon Salzberg

As long as we are alive,
an exquisite infinity of motion
moves through us, and we through it.
This is incarnation.
The greatest blessing is to choose to savor our embodiment.
— Dunya, from a talk at the 2020 Embodiment Conference

INTRODUCTION

In Dancemeditation, dance is the doorway in, not out.
Dancemeditation shines the body's light into the shadowed self.
— Dunya

I spread my blanket in the teaching spot at the front of the room, set-up
the music for today's session, place my journal beside me, and heap a
graceful silk veil nearby. My students arrive bit by bit. They arrange their
blankets of varied colors and textures in sloppy arcs facing mine. Gentle
music cushions the air between us. The room's ambience softens. We each
turn away from whatever we have been doing and toward where we are
now, finding our breathing, feeling gravity's tug in this space with its light
and smells and temperature. It is time to begin.

What is beginning? Journalist and somatics expert, Jae Grunek, wrote
about my class for *NYSpirit Magazine*. I think it captures the first brush
with Dancemeditation.

The Sense of Moving: The Feeling of Me

We begin the class nearly reclining, timing our inhalations and exhalations to
the quiet, rhythmic music. We follow Dunya's lead, repeating a sequence of gentle
stretches that alters and deepens bit by bit. My body begins to lengthen, awaken,
and relax. Dunya hardly speaks, and the atmosphere in the classroom becomes
thick with the attention we pay to our languorous movements.

Dunya's guided warm-up transitions comfortably into an individual one with the instruction to close our eyes and move any way we like. I continue the luxurious stretching on the floor, following my impulses as I become fascinated in the differences between my right and left sides.

I sneak a peek at the rest of the room and see that, truly, everyone has found a unique way of dancing. Some have risen to their feet. Many play with their natural posture and gestures I recognize from before the class began. Looking at them, I want nothing other than to go back to what is as uniquely mine as their movements are theirs. So I close my eyes again...

I feel myself move more delicately than I am wont, with all the qualities of a string of pearls: light, luminous, rounded, and refined. Eventually I wear myself out and settle against a wall to watch the other students. Curiously, their movements seem to shed my gaze as a tent sheds water. Though they're bared for me to see by the way they move, the significance of those movements is theirs alone, and I can't divine it.

At last Dunya invites us all to rest on our back for a final long repose. The music plays softly in the background, and the memory of my dancing plays through my body just below the level of my conscious mind.

I tell Dunya later that, for an ostensibly spiritual undertaking, I'd found her class surprisingly grounded in physical realities. She explained the class is an evolving form developed from her background in dance, yoga, and the Sufi tradition she taught for many years. "I want to help my students go beyond habitualness to something that is happening right now... to come to a sense of relaxation and self-trust, and feel more connected to their whole body self. There is nothing, in terms of spiritual pursuit, that should go away from the body."

At the time, that was my response to Jae. Now I would include that because body is spirit we cannot actually ever go away from it. In Dancemeditation, an embodied mysticism, dance *is* the meditation. I define mysticism as moving through deepening states of consciousness into the Moment, and body as the fabric of consciousness. Body moves. Body is movement. Body is consciousness. In Dancemeditation, the subject of this volume, we move and dance, seeking and discovering who and what we are.

Finding My Mysticism

In childhood, I was a little mystic, as children often are, and I loved to dance and play music and draw, as children do. I was in the Moment. I was connected to the All. As I grew up, I increasingly lost track of my innermost self and my connection to All. My familial world was quite alive with mystical threads, but school education was the suppression of self-realization in favor of social conditioning. I felt the gradual alienation most in dance, my primary language, since whatever was truly worth my knowing went through that lens.

Western education emphasizes the mastery of information; to become adept in a field—in my case dance—one trains, attains expertise, then performs and teaches the art form. I enjoyed it. It was fun. It was a puzzle, and the puzzles got harder and more complex, but always a sort of game for my mind or my body, which were handled as separate parts of me. I attended Juilliard and went on to perform professionally, choreograph to critical acclaim, and teach at universities, always seeking and not finding that shimmering, immense timelessness I'd known as a child.

At 29 years old, a NYC concert artist with a thriving career, I struggled with a difficult physical injury. This was 1980, before the internet and early in the burgeoning Human Potential Movement. A fellow dancer told me about a Shattari Sufi master, Adnan Sarhan from Baghdad, traveling through, giving workshops. "It's physically easy," she said. "There is this really fabulous energy," she said. So one evening I accompanied her to the Little Red Schoolhouse in Lower Manhattan snd plunked down on a carpeted floor amidst one hundred other people seated side-by-side.

I had no background in meditation and few expectations. We all faced a stage to follow a little, stocky, older man's movements and, in very short order, a syrupy, golden-ish energy flooded into me. No words, no explanations, no corrections, no acquisition. Yet oddly familiar. I picked right up from where I'd left off in childhood, as if the intervening years were irrelevant. This was what I had yearned for. The mystery in my depths said *Yes*.

Sufi was a rich field of inner-facing movement. Words were sparingly employed and even seemed to be a hindrance to mystical experience; so I let go of my mental edifices, opening to a new sort of knowledge swirling through me. The word for this conveyance of knowledge between teacher and student which ignites the student's awakening is 'transmission.' I felt I was swimming in an elemental, reciprocal flux activated at a cellular level.

For 17 years I continued to attend long retreats and workshops. The experiences there transformed me, the way heat transforms ice into water then steam—not a 'get better,' 'be wiser' sort of way, but as a leavening which washed out my starch, rendering me fluid and connected to a continually shifting holism. I was finally waking up inside my life.

I thought that to go from open-eyed, expressive performance—a relationship between myself and others—to closed-eyed inward-faced dance ending the I/you duality was the only shift I needed in order to be fulfilled. Then teaching brought me to the next evolution.

The Elephant in the Room

I was steeped in three capacious fields that I loved—Art, the evanescent realm of Aesthetics and Expression; Somatics, the awakening of embodied awareness; and Mysticism, the uniquely personal sense of relationship to the Beyond. When I set out to teach, I continued in the footsteps of those who had come before me, teaching what I knew as I had learned it, and seeing what would happen. I wasn't yet trying to make something different.

It seems, if I try to generalize, that I drew on Western sources for their color and texture and their ability to inspire and unlock the body-being's imaginal capacities; on Somatics for healing—I was usually there to mend from injury—and deepening embodiment; the underlying mystical field of awareness came from Sufi methods which hypnotize and entrain. All three sources rested on body-denying assumptions which I accepted, though in time these began to niggle.

Western dance is physically grueling and abusive to the body—a *tour de force* of criticism and correction in order to manifest desirable artistic forms. Sufi, in its charge towards transcendence, carries an implied dismissal of the physical plane in general, a feature of the centuries-old mind/body schism privileging mind as spiritual and body as base. Somatics is driven by the therapeutic model that justifies body connection for the sake of improvement, a soft sort of correction. All three sought to externally alter me in more or less punitive ways since even Somatics, a healthful modality, rested on the premise of injury as weakness or disability or moral failing. These were the past and not where Dancemeditation was going.

Teaching brought up questions, and I slowly took inventory. By now, with plenty of time on the mat and time under my belt, I felt ready to respect my misgivings. Something at the core of each modality on its own fell short. The elephant in the room was the body. It was through teaching, informed by my exploratory daily practice—a personal laboratory—that a fundamental reconceptualizing of body roiled and bubbled up from my cells. Dancemeditation began to emerge.

A Long, Messy Birth

I wish I could say that Dancemeditation arrived with a nice clear ting. Instead I struggled in mess and murk. It took time to actually *feel* inside my own intimate skin. As I crawled through increasingly fraught territory, it was difficult to have confidence in myself, to trust myself.

Concerning body and spirit, none of the root traditions agreed with me. They maintained that body was a glass holding the water of spirit while in my experience we are glass and water combined. Eventually the rift between body and spirit collapsed; it became clear that body is the fabric of consciousness. This may seem an easy blip of words, but inside a body blunted by cultural misinformation, the journey is anything but trivial.

We have all been schooled to distrust or revile our body. I believe this rift is the source of our misery. When divorced from our body, we are not cradled in resonance with nature, nor content with the gifts of existence —Earth, sky, animals, fellow humans. We are unable to rest in communion with the Moment.

Once we know that our body is the fabric of consciousness, we can move in this fabric into deeper states of consciousness and into a connection bound neither by time nor culturally constructed myths. We are pure experience of existence. With this singing in every cell, I've relaxed into a world of discovery. Dancemeditation continually, creatively alters itself. Less potent elements slough away, core materials gravitate together and synthesize into a distinct, singular process that retains rich and beloved roots but is greater than its birthing parts. I follow the very fine gold thread spooling out from my being into what can just barely be seen up ahead.

Naming

The words 'meditation' and 'dance' frequently congeal in narrow, oppositional memes—meditation is sitting still, and dance is moving around—and what most of us know about dance, what I knew as well until entering the great ocean of mysticism, is three shoddy little shacks perched on the beach: Performance Dance, Fitness Dance, Social Dance. The shacks are crowded, noisy, smelly, teaming with fractious bargaining.

We walk out of the shacks and step to the lip of the ocean where waves stroke the sand. We wade in to our ankles, our knees, hips, until we slide forward, our feet peeling from the ground, to be swallowed in swells and salt and freedom, carried away from noise and effort into enormity.

We move in any direction, floating, paddling, stroking. There is no how we must float, how we must paddle, how we must stroke. In this watery magnitude, we neither drive ourselves nor sleep through the wonderment. This is Dancemeditation—dance this deep.

Dance has always been deep. In early Earth eons, humans imitated creatures and natural geological forms to connect, to be like, to be infused with. One danced like the wolf to be inhabited by the spirit of the wolf. Dervishes whirled to align with the cosmos. Dances were not decorative; they intersected and interrupted and interwove with existence. Though over the years I have spent a lot of energy defending the full depth of dance, it truly needs no such champion. It is the body's language and the language of matter, and all of us who close our eyes and sink within to move understand this.

The Dancemeditation practice I teach nestles within a larger field of embodied mysticism. Neither mysticism nor body are esoteric; they are here, right now. The name I chose, which is plain and simple, is from my own language and helped me claim and inhabit my Path, as well as deal with repressive imprints from my own culture without having to lug around antiquated relics from other traditions that dismiss or oppress the body.

Moving & Awakening

Our modern life demands that we sit too much in front of computers and in vehicles, physically repressed and emotionally and mentally overstimulated. Most of us report feeling stress, malaise, depression, and illness. Meditation has become an important balance, yet systems that work only in stillness are less effective against sedentary daily assault. We need to de-stimulate *and* we need to move. The simple, natural, noncompetitive, embodying movement meditations in this book helps us gently focus and unwind.

Dancemeditations soothe our nervous system, support our endocrine system, gently pump our circulatory and lymphatic systems, and hydrate our interstitium, all of which lessens the anxieties that relentlessly plague us whether from internal or external woes. On the physical and emotional planes alone it is tremendous support. I offer these not as a pitch or promise or a trick to get us into a consumerist state of mind, but rather to state the obvious. Of course embodiment will redress disconnections dinned into us by discombobulating culture, and of course Dancemeditation, which balances levels of stimulation—mostly, in this current era, calming overstimulation—will help us feel better. Most important, by relaxing us, helping us feel safe in our body, Dancemeditation gives us our ground to know creativity and wonderment. Carl G. Jung, psychiatrist, psychologist, and founder of analytical psychology, said, "When the great swing has taken an individual into the world of symbolic mysteries, nothing comes of it, nothing can come of it, unless it has been associated with the earth, unless it has happened when that individual was in the body...first return to the body, to your earth." I would add, return there moving. Moving meditation is a graspable, doable, effective, immediate pursuit.

The Beyond

What seems to be true and enduring for most seekers is that a daily or regular conscious observation of internal experience offers distance from immediate reactivity. Whether a daily practice requires a deity or faith is an individual matter. Path or practice needn't rest upon a sense of the Evanescent, though I think most seekers share a glimmer that existence extends beyond personal identity toward a universal field of awareness. During my own journey, I've volleyed from believing in a ready-made god, to crafting for myself a uniquely personal god, to having no god except Nature, ending most of the time in a confusion concerning scale —*I am so small and something, but What?, is so very great!*—only to have this duality melt away. And so it goes, over and back, but I know that I spiral ever closer to a sense of pure experience for which philosophical definition is less necessary. I am comfortable in my being.

I mention this in order to say that I have no opinion for others on this aspect of the search; however, I have never found this to be an impediment to sharing the search. As one Sufi friend said, "Who am I to define your mysticism?" Yes, mine is mine, and yours is yours. All our goddesses, gods, and nons- get along. Seeking happens within, and we can support one another simply by going forth side-by-side, sometimes in tandem, keeping each other company.

Meeting on the Path

Those I meet who have a Path are spurred on by two things, either one or the other or antiphonally—yearning and pain. Though the wish to escape pain can be motivating, it is yearning that turns us into seekers. Yearning, and by this I mean an inchoate river running, often quietly, beneath all of our wanting, is mysterious. We tend to feel it far inside and meet it coming to face us in unexpected flashes. Yearning and seeking inform this volume, and I hope I provide what I've most valued in my reading on my Path which is a sense of companionship, rather than dogma, for when I inevitably feel lonely or lose my way.

As I write, I have had in mind since the outset those who regularly practice movement meditation in solitude, or those who would like to. I also write for those who hear or see the words 'dance' and 'meditation' either combined as I use them, or following one after the other with a space in between, and would like an introduction to this version of the pursuit. The clearest inspiration has been those who've been practicing this largely nonverbal body of work with me over the past several decades and might be relieved to have a few words as confirmation, as contemplation, as support, and perhaps, finally, as thoughtful understanding of what they have been doing. In truth, I write for any person who would like to embrace their body as an intimate, safe home and a realm of wonderment.

Last but not least, I write it for myself to help me think about what I feel in my practice, a work I have spent a lifetime delving into, which has cultivated me, created me, and dissolved me in the hopes of honoring in at least one small human way a truly infinite and treasured Path.

ABOUT THE PHOTOGRAPHS

With a couple of exceptions, the photographs in this book are an evocative body of work by master dance photographer Paul B. Goode. They are of The Alembic, a performance project group of dancers gathered together in NYC studying Dancemeditation with me intensively for their own healing and development. The Alembic offered meditations intended to be publicly witnessed by audiences as a way to grow as performers, deepening their capacity for being seen while sharing the field of interiority the practice engenders. The project spanned about two years. Performance events took place in the Metropolitan Building, a magnificent art space in a warehouse in Queens, NYC designed and directed by Eleanor Ambos.

Part One
ABODE

Making a sanctuary
to support our exploration

MAKING THE SANCTUARY

Some of us come to mystical seeking drawn by an inscrutable yearning—a whisper, a shout, a persistent gnawing. We yearn for what we don't know. Others of us fall into it by accident, not knowing until we are there that this exceptional yet wholly natural beauty exists. So, we come. We pass into the Mystery and know we are home. A taste may become a practice. A practice may become a Path. The Mystery nudges us to fashion a nest—a place and time for rummaging in the treasures of being-ness. Our abode.

Our seeking may be accompanied or solitary, infrequent or regular, but its situation has specific attributes. An abode is safe. It is sequestered. It is uninterrupted. It is not obligated. It is intimate. As phenomenologist, Gaston Bachelard, wrote in his beautiful treatise, *The Poetics of Space*, "There does not exist an intimacy that is repellant." The surroundings are its bones. Its time frame, mediated by music and quiet, is the auditory enclosure. And then, there is the invitation—the self invites our Self. A part of us must hold out its hand inviting our totality to the dance.

Of course, despite the call in my heart, I also forget or hesitate or resist. I am continually entangled in phenomena. Sufi poet, Jallaludin Rumi, remarks that phenomena steal our essence. I must work my way back again and again to my abode where I nest my seeking. I'm sure I am not alone in this. What can we do? Will power, as we have all probably experienced, is not terribly effective. It is practically useless against the confluence of friction that accumulates to prevents us. Friction is often our downfall.

Such a little word, but it deserves our notice; we will need to outwit friction to make it easier to be in what we love, to enter the heart of our Heart. What is friction? Simple things. Having to move too many things out of the way in order to put down your mat. Having to dig up what to wear each time; a lot of practice sessions have gotten lost as we hunt through our closets. Not having helpful music at the ready. This sort of thing. Removing friction is not in itself very deep. It may even seem trivial, but I like to think of it as a bridge over the moat. We really need that bridge to get into the castle. Time spent on our abode, minimizing the 'friction' between wanting to do what we want to do and doing it, is a powerful ally.

We each will find our own space and way. It is part of learning who we are and what we need, and this will change as we change. I like to think of my abode, which over time has developed and refined itself, as carved out of purity. Here are a few things to consider.

1 PLACE

I found a nest in the skeleton of the ivy
A soft nest of country moss and dream herb.
— Yvan Goll

A sanctuary space embraces you. It fits you. I'll borrow from Bachelard his description of a bird pressing her breast again and again along the inner wall of her nest, making a nest that is the shape of her. The room needn't be overlay large—no bigger that the full kinesphere, the space our body takes up when arms and legs are fully stretched in any direction. Clean is important. A clean space with a clean rug or mat that is warm in winter and cool in summer allows our body to fully relax. A dedicated area for your use alone—a separate room, a cabin, or a portion of an art studio or creative space—is extremely helpful. Good ventilation is important.

Always have a simple sound system ready—an iPod, or a phone (in airplane mode so you are not tempted to check it). Find the most comforting set of 'vestments' to use just for practice made of natural fabrics in colors that soothe you with layers to adjust temperature as the body cools or warms. In short, something you look forward to putting on. Leave a clean set in the practice sanctuary to avoid the what-to-wear procrastination and don't wear these particular ones for anything else. In addition, a journal for noting your experience at the end can provide a harmonious transition back from wordlessness.

A home studio is an opportunity to weave together our practice and our daily life, while having a practice room outside our home leads us through a larger world context when coming and going. Each choice has benefits and challenges, and if our practice persists through time, we will very likely experience both settings.

For those of us initiating regular practice during a nomadic phase, all these parameters exist 'on the road.' I once did a six week cross-country drive, sleeping in the guest rooms of friends or in the back of my small SUV at campgrounds. At one park, I spread my blanket on a picnic table because the ground was too rocky. I didn't miss a day; my blanket and clothing were my abode.

Two Places, Two Possibilities

My Sufi teacher had a mundane teaching spot—his only practice spot since he taught full time and had no need for a solo practice. At Sufi Camp, he taught from a raised wooden platform covered by ugly mustard-colored wall-to-wall carpeting. Along one side marched a tidy line-up of sound equipment and boxes of cassette tapes. Behind hung a plaque with the calligraphy of the Sufi chant *La illaha ilallah* which means There is no God but God. A plain, basic scene, no gold or fluted columns. He sat on a serviceable orange and blue-patterned beach towel purchased at Target. Every couple of weeks at the end of the workshop, he slung it around his neck and took it to be laundered. When it wore thin, someone mended it.

Over the seventeen Sufi Summer Camp years I attended, he only once replaced this towel. He wore the same outfit when teaching––white yoga pants and a T-shirt. He owned several of these. (For traveling or shopping he had one, and only one, uniform.) He was sufficiently well groomed. The same aesthetic held true for workshop rooms. His Sufi Camp in New Mexico—a former youth camp constructed from donated ex-military windows and cements blocks—was humble, drab, yet serviceable, relying on the high desert mountain nature setting with its pure air and temperate summers for beauty and magic. He didn't need much, except the work and minimal support for those of us training with him. You might be this minimalist sort as well.

What do I like? I require a bit more. My practice room is an altar; the surroundings are as much a devotion as my motion. For me, teaching is periodic. The majority of time in my Path is solitary, regular practice. I like the same basics as those in which I trained––clean, quiet, and a good temperature. I don't need an ascetic room, though I dislike clutter. I love simple beauty that is neither forbidding nor cold—a room that invites me into its warmth. I spend time with this, moving the vase of flowers a little to the left, stacking folded blankets neatly, putting pillows in a large woven basket. The objects need to sit so comfortably that they almost disappear, much the way I also hope to be myself. Texture and color matter. This placing of objects satisfies part of my artistic nature. Though I won't see the room during most of my movement time, I will see this visual grace before I close my eyes to begin and when I open them at the end. It is like a theatre experience in reverse: the audience starts the journey in darkness, light then illuminates the play, and at the end the lights go out. In practice, I start in the light and note that even the most beautiful room appears stiff, dense, ungracious. I then close my eyes, extinguishing the outer light. At the end, I open my eyes to the return of light and to a metamorphosis. The air has a honeyed glow flecked with a barely discernible sparkling. Distances and shapes harmonize. Sufis call this *wudad*—the 'love in this space.'

Objects and Smells

The objects in the space exert a surprising yet subtle influence. I prefer not to have random books or devices requiring my attention; their presence seems to nag from the periphery, "Come here and finish!" I am discomforted by sofas with spiders under their skirts or a forest of spindly chair legs. If I have to move a table to make room to roll and stretch, it seems disgruntled that I've stolen its spot and waits impatiently for me to finish. The blare of a lightbulb's naked haunch glimpsed from beneath its shade from my spot on the floor is faintly shaming, as if I've been caught looking up its knickers. The dust beneath radiators and baseboards is unseen in upright life, but once prone I discover its seclusion; I invade its privacy so it spews a bit of itself toward me in discouragement. I've pruned these attention seekers in my space because, though objects may appear inanimate, they have lives and being-ness we mustn't underestimate. Their utilitarian existence might infuse practice with an excess of distracting information.

I have a horror of bad smells. Bad smells are, in simple actuality, teeny weeny particles of rotting or burning or noxious things sucked on the inhale into nose and lungs. On the other hand, the scent of the stargazer lily opens an inner heaven.

Touch, Sheepskins, Veils

Whatever touches my skin matters to my inner world. I wrap in warm womb-ness, in a protective nest of wool, cotton, and silk, undisturbed by insects or phone calls, frigid drafts or someone bursting through the door. Sheepskins are an old Sufi thing. They are some sort of perfect. I remember attending a *zhikr* —a chanting ceremony—with the Helveti Jerrahi order in NYC in the 1980s. The word *zhikr* means 'remembrance' and means the remembering of one's true essence. Three musicians sat in the center of the room surrounded by members of the Sufi order. We guests sat in concentric rings around this nucleus. The Sufis spent the first hour setting up, coming in and out of the room, laughing and chatting, excited anticipation in the air. Toss a sheepskin down, then go away, then come back, move several skins, tuck a new one between, rearrange again. Apparently there was a skin for each Sufi—place mats at the *zhikr* table. Finally everyone sat, and the *zhikr* happened, and it was fantastic and wild and powerful. On sheepskins.

For the past few years I have depended on sheepskins at my remote retreat property which has no furnace. When temperatures abruptly drop, I stoke the wood stove and curl up on their coziness. In the cold, damp bone-chill of coastal Cape Cod winter, sheepskins are soft and warm as I roll on the floor, and when standing, allow my feet to connect with the ground. Each skin, like the animal in its living time, has its own personality. They are still alive to me, pulsing with unique qualities, and convey a guardian angel guidance. Sheep and lambs rescue me from fraying and fragmenting, encourage tactile explorations, absorb upwellings of grief, and soothe trauma. Soft things. Gentle things.

Silk veils. I dance with them. I rest warmly under them. I drape them around my shoulders to protect my seated chanting. I use them as straps when I stretch. They adorn any meditation spot with beauty. They fold into lightweight packets for traveling. As well, since I have painted my own with silk dye, they contain my creative intuitive time. I have three ultra long ones, two regular length ones, and two short ones. Three of any kind seems to be the most I allow myself because I value being able to care for everything that lives in my life. Too many belongings risk being forgotten, neglected, abandoned.

Clothing

Of course we all know what we like to wear, but from time to time it is worthwhile to review the choices and make sure they feel right. Even if we share our practice time with others, for the most part we are working with closed eyes, so feeling is more important than looks. Personally, I've learned that I can't tolerate anything girdle-esque. No lycra. Conversely, I find entangling swathes of fabric as annoying as a small yipping dog; while I roll and move I must rise up from my inner depths to fuss. A soft, fairly close top and Indian patiala that narrow in at the ankle with blouson thighs are perfect. They don't slide up to my knees when I'm in Shoulder Stand nor catch my feet when I dance about. I feel them lightly ring below my belly, never across my viscera or pushing at the bottom edge of my diaphragm. As well, they never, ever grab my crotch. They're made of cotton or linen for summer and silk for cooler times. These are my vestments. The color choices shift from the to time, but without exception I wear natural fibers.

Undisturbed

An intimate, creative, safe relationship with self prospers when we are available to ourself (and not to others) for the duration of our practice. Whether you practice in wilderness, a village, suburb, or a megalopolis, reduce or eliminate interruptions. Turn off your phone. Make sure pets are happy and out of your way, and, for humans, hang up the Do Not Disturb sign. This time is a journey inside self with no other obligation.

How ever spacious, [place] must also be a cottage, a dove-cote, a nest, a chrysalis.
Intimacy needs the heart of a nest.
Erasmus, his biographer tells us, was long "in finding a nook in his fine house
in which he could put his little body with safety."
— Gaston Bachelard, *Poetics of Space*

2 REGULARITY, DURATION, MUSIC

My body is the book of me, the book of my world, the book of my human history. My dance is a quill writing.
— Dunya

Regularity

Regular practice provides perspective which, in my book, is a large measure of sanity. The meditations themselves are salubrious, but the true power of practice is the *reliability* of being less alarmed, which helps us stop taking every immediate drama as forever and always. We are, on a regular basis, a sane person. This trustworthiness gives our life a stabilizing through-line. I regard my own spiritual seeking as a lifelong project. A project is not an incident; it is a continuum with varied stages and ways; it has duration and repetition. As well, a project is not an accident: it is chosen. Most important, this lifelong project is something I do, not something I am, thus I can engage in it regardless of the distance or nearness to my perceived sense of self. I wrote this about my daily practice in *Skin of Glass*, my memoir:

Each morning practice is a small picture frame placed at about eye level, or third eye level, or some days at belly button level. I look into an empty frame and the stream of me unfolds, curls, explodes. These frames placed side by side, day by day, form a movie of embodiment. In the continuum I murmur, "I am changing again..." Thoughts become very loose and light because I see, over and over, again that they come and go. They are nothing much—zephyrs, whispers. My thought-delineated identity has the feel of a flowered cotton curtain that's been hanging in the sun so long it is faded and threadbare. Now passing flies knock holes in it. Obstacles dwindle and there's beauty. The wide pleasure.

Regularity is sculpted out of repetition. Since we do repetitious practices nested in a repetition of practice sessions, our feelings about, and capacity with, repetition itself is central to our pursuit of awakening. Repetition plucks us out of a flighty escapist sky—that fast getaway from the big mess in which we are embroiled—and tempers expectations of salvation. To face into repetition is to know the engine of our seeking.

For some of us, probably all of us at one time or another, repetition has had a bad taste. Repetition seems like bars on a cage when we are caught in the frustration of intransigent habits or the sameness of a dull job or relationship. Naturally, we have forgotten pleasurable repetitious: coming home to our dog's reliable enthusiasm, the annual bloom of daffodils, or the daily morning cup of coffee. Those repetitions are reassuring. When experience feels good, we notice, and in the noticing perceive the variation. *The daffodils have never been so yellow! Our dog's every wag and sniffle pings in our heart.* Much of our suffering comes from lack of noticing. Repetition in meditation involves copious amounts of noticing.

Though repetition implies exactitude, it is more like a stand of birches, its chorus of similarity full of subtle differences. Every day we do practices on our mat and pay attention and as excitement and boredom level out, attentiveness reveals beauty. We put step after step, breath after breath, dance after dance, discovering that things aren't so bad, and when they are bad we know that we can manage. This is sanity.

Dancemeditation Is This Ocean

Out of the deep blue, an incoming curl hisses over a lip of red-umber eel grass, then sucks back, chewing on barnacles and dragging pebbles, the sound like a bony roll of ten thousand dice. The sea has been beach combing, digesting the shore, and thirty feet out under a watery veil, makes a milky sand bar of its findings. The bar swoons and stirs at every tidal tug. Insistent caress. Dancemeditation is this ocean: a ceaseless roil across the gravel of pain, wearing it down, until we are only pure fluid response to Cosmic Breath.

—Dunya, journal entry

Duration

I once saw a squirrel perched on its hindquarters on a rock cliff gazing down a long wilderness canyon, perfectly still and serene. He appeared to be engaged in a contemplative state, though I may anthropomorphizing. He sat for 10 minutes. I have come to think of this as a squirrel-length meditation duration. Humans, who are bigger and slower, need longer. Levity aside, we humans need 20 minutes to downshift our neurotransmitter bath, that is, going from being awash in cortisol to turning on the serotonin, dopamine, and endorphin taps that soak our tissues in calmer biochemistry. Then, once we are calm, it is pleasant to have at least another 5 or 10 minutes for enjoyment. I like to have 45 — 90 minutes and use music as my auditory timer. That's duration, but remember, the squirrel also chose a nice quiet, uninterrupted spot. (I like to think he knew I was a kindred soul and wouldn't disturb him.) Take his cue. Pre-empt potential disruptions before you begin so you can be available to yourself (and not to others) for the practice duration.

Music

Music is a forcefield. Music is a guide. Music creates time. Music is a room in the room—a nook, a womb, a castle, a cave, a world so resonant our physics are altered. Music is the containment and the guide. Music leads our cells. Music measures the room. We close our eyes, relinquishing outer visuality, and our hearing grows more acute. Our ears orient us in the space, acoustically calculating distance between our body and the wall, the floor, the ceiling. Music modulates this spatial fabric. As well, music is more than meets the ears. Our skin reads air pressure, humidity, and temperature in part by how the sound moves through the air in the space. Music cradles us in time. The right music also transforms our perception of time making time irrelevant, even stopping time. Knowing this, when we seek music for inner journey, we prosper from supportive choices. The paramount principal is to choose not from the head, nor even from the heart, but from closer into the flesh. Deep Dancing and Imaginal Realm Movement mark two spectrum ends of our musical sustenance. Where our Imaginal Realm thrives on variation and inspiration, music for Deep Dancing invites quietude and entrains us into meditative states.

Music for Deep Dancing

Music for deep work is not an entertainment. Music for deep dancing is spacious. What does this mean? Often the compositions are an attenuated continuum with evolutionary, shifting moods and few abrupt changes. The music is either unmetered or a slow tempo. Because our heartbeat aligns with any rhythm line we hear, a slower percussion line or meter slows out heart rate. Unmetered music, or an elasticity within an overall steady meter—the word for this is *rubato*—leads away from the sense of rushing and rigidity and towards a luxuriant timelessness. Repetition in incantatory melody lines lull us, or the lines may meander like a vine without beginning or end, winding back and forth until we forget where we began or where we are going. Music lush with ornamentation pauses to flower within the progression, as if we stop along the woodsy path where a shrub blooms.

It is not difficult to find extraordinarily subtle, profound, beautiful, evocative music for inward journey. Many cultures have a well-developed contemplative musical literature. Classical Indian, Arabic, Persian, Turkish, and Gregorian chant to name a few. These rich traditions propitiate meditative entrainment. Start here. It is already well-mapped. As well, the musicians themselves know how to sink in and traverse deep, non-ordinary states.

We can experientially appreciate this music, but I think understanding how it achieves its purpose is worth knowing. Most of the above-mentioned contemplative musical traditions use chordal structure sparingly if at all. (Chords are single tones stacked on top of one another, vibrating against one another to create an aural density.) For our meditative purposes this lack of density is interesting to consider. Typically, contemplative music employs a drone (the tamboura in Indian music is one example), or a repeated a pulse called *ostinato* (the *chiftetelli* in Arabic music) which acts a stable through-line—a sonic background. An individual instrument unfolds its journey above this background. This creates spacious sound. Even when multiple instruments play together, rather than precision chordal harmony, they go along in a loose unison, like a group of friends walking together down a road. Again, spaciousness.

The overall compositional or improvisational structures vary as well. If you think of the themes and variations of Western music which invoke meaning by starting us somewhere, moving us away, then returning, you'll note how much aural information we take in. It is a cerebral, intellectual, and emotional pleasure. By comparison, Eastern music is evolutionary, unfolding bit by bit. We may end up far away from where we began and it doesn't matter since we never have to remember what came before where we are now. Our analytical minds are quieted. We are drawn to the present moment. That alone is a powerful emphasis. But something more fundamental is at the core of musical spaciousness.

I once had a fascinating conversation with my friend, master oud player, Joe Zeytoonian, about overtones—those bell-like pings that come from touching a vibrating string. (An oud is the precursor to Western lute, the latter's name coming from the Arabic *el oud.*) The gist was that overtones enter and resonate within our tissues and bones, plucking us the way a guitar string is plucked. Moreover, the lower down on the overtone sequence the music, the more easily our being digests the tone. Well, I loved thinking about the actual physics of music, not just aesthetics. He went on to explain more about how overtones sound at intervals above the base tone—thus 'overtone'.

The first interval above the base tone, the octave, is most distant. That distance makes it the most spacious interval. It is also the most consonant. It is strong and solid to our ears. The farther up one goes, the more closely the overtones cluster. Diverse cultures use different tones, called notes, as well as different arrangements of notes, called scales. These differences are what characterize different musics, but for all music, the intervals emanate from the overtones, called the harmonic overtone sequence.

Joe pointed out that the pentatonic drones and ragas of classical Indian music as well as the *maqams* (modal scales) of Arabic and Persian music reside lower down on the overtone sequence making them more spacious in how they vibrate, and this in turn makes them easier for our flesh to digest. "The octave, the 4th and 5th settle well in the ear." And we both agreed that they also settle well in the body. The vibrations organize our cells into a grounded alignment with one another, settling our cells. This creates a sense of spaciousness. While Eastern music is not at all simple—it is highly ornamental and microtonally complex—it is experientially spacious. (Western music employs minimalism to deliver aural spaciousness—a sense that the music is moving while going nowhere—which, though hypnotic, is not the same vibratory process.)

These technical understandings are important to articulate because—I'll say it again—music is a forcefield. Music plays us. Music moves in our bones. Music, literally, moves us and that movement is immensely subtle. One music is not better than another, but they have different purposes. Choosing music for deepening is not merely a matter of taste or of triggering emotional association, choices which come from a more cerebral listening strata closer to thought. For dancing deeply, we need music that moves away from complexity and directly into our flesh. Since it will be our primary embrace for an hour, returning again and again to a few well-chosen pieces helps us know we are safely home. We don't need a million choices. We need just a few pieces we can rest into, trusting them to carry us from the superficial to the subtle.

Music for Our Imaginal Realm

Deepening comes in many ways. Our bodybeing deepens when we let it play and dream. In contrast to music for Deep Dancing, for our body's imaginative exploration, we need a variety of music and music that is new to us, varied in mood, tempo, cultural flavors and savors. We need yummy fare for our tissues because our bodyself deepens when we let it play and dream. For those who like to move into deeper states in fast tempo, drumming will be the anchor. Repetitive percussion carries us along. For letting our flesh explore and dream, plangent, bouncy, sexy, heart-warming are just few adjectives. That said, we don't want anything abrasive or over-anxious. And we can do without music which is trying to seduce us with its cleverness, its busy-ness. Because we are deepening beyond emotion into our essential energy, music that plucks heartstrings or manipulates our emotions is unhelpful.

Lyrics and the Word Trap

We love a song which has a little lyric in the middle, something like "I am your slave.' When we are making the mix we've been reading a lot of Rumi and know that this means we are slave to God or Divine Love and think the lyric, though we understand English and it is in English, won't disturb us because it is spiritual. Then, we are in our practice, going along and the we hear "I am your slave." We aren't thinking about Rumi, or the poets. We haven't been thinking anything at all but suddenly we think 'slave to what?' Or just 'slave,' which sounds not so good and then, at last, the Rumi bit comes back to our mind and we remember why we had included that song in the mix. During all this retrieval, we have been moving, not feeling what we are doing, and up in our heads. Now the lyrics finish, instrumental music returns, and now we have to drop down in again. So that's how it is with lyrics in our own language: we know what they mean, our mind picks up on them, hijacking our efforts to suspend random thinking and muddying our efforts to stay in sensory connection to our body. Veer away from lyrics in your own language. A little may be fine— fragmentary, amusing, undemanding phrases that come and go without derailing us.

About Silences

Silence is a sound space.

The occasional silence in deep dancing often enters our attenuated time sense as a perfect place to breathe deeply, to unwind. In music from the contemplative traditions, silences are few, come at the right moment, and are the right length of time, as if taking a long sigh before the next utterance. In a way, they aren't true silences as much as suspended pauses arcing very quietly with very little motion from one place to another. We are never sonically dropped.

For exploring the imaginal realm, we build a music journey with a variety of moods. Compile a sequence—you are a DJ now—dovetailing tracks, growing one from the other with some sort of logic. If, for example, you are connecting them through tempo, song succession may increase then decrease in tempo. Or perhaps adjacent songs are in the same key, or one has a strong vocal so the next has no vocal. Choose your order, then get into a music mixing program and crossfade the tracks. Remember, silence is a sound space. In the context of music for the imaginal realm, silence feels like a cue to stop what we are doing. When collating a musical journey for exploratory play, remove the dead air. This is important, whether you are shaping mood-shifts or a soundscape of seamless trance-y burbling (which John Schaefer, host of WNYC's excellent *New Sounds* experimental new music show calls 'music with movement that doesn't go anywhere'). My Sufi teacher, Adnan Sarhan, laughingly, but in all seriousness, called silences in the dance music places for the devil to come in. Which points to a crucial factor: we always want to help our mind drop obsessive, controlling thoughts. A continuous sound bath drowns mental perseveration.

lure

patience

invitation

inclusiveness

open

3 THE LURE, PATIENCE, INVITATION, INCLUSIVENESS, OPEN

My blood is alive with the many voices
telling me I am made of longing.
— Rilke, *Rilke's Book of Hours*

On our mat, we cultivate openness, being-ness, and a nonjudgmental Inner Witness. This doesn't mean we have to achieve this or even intend it. I am not a great proponent of intentions because, like a gun, we can so easily turn them against us. Intentions morph into tyrants. However, I am quite certain that a more wondrous self-relationship is inevitable by the simple act of showing up on the mat and the employment of a few attitudinal parameters. One, it helps to remember the lure. What draws you there? Two, patience. We must always have patience. It helps to regard patience as a lovely, spacious field of wonder. Three, because creatures prefer sweet to bitter, invitations work better than commands. Four, inclusiveness. Five, being open.

The Lure

For most people the lure is something along these lines. Ordinary worlds disappear. In the airy, pulsing sanctuary, in the temple of music and motion, whisperings bubble up from behind our back, from beneath our radar, from beyond our ken. It is an hour of secrets when we are not wrong. Pure. In the way of ice to water, water to mist, mist to water to ice, we move, reaching in. The skirt of Infinity brushes a swirling hem through us. Just keep remembering the lure.

Patience

My father was a marine biologist. This way of being didn't stop when he stepped away from his microscope. It was how he met the world of both marine and terrestrial creatures, great and small. One warm summer day in Maine, we walked to a cove-like curve of shoreline all boulders and hand-sized rocks rubbed smooth by sucking tides. We were drawn there by the raucous cries of hundreds of seagulls wheeling overhead. Gulls congregate to nest and socialize in favorite spots which they coat in guano, but they are just as likely to convene in a one-off location like that rocky beach. Gulls flew in and out, different sizes and colorations, juvenile to adult as well as different species. The whirring above us! The cacophony around us!

More and more arrived and found perches. My father and I settled ourselves on the warm stones to watch. Jostling, jeers, pecking, food sharing, food stealing, invectives, and chortling. Some relationships were amicable, and others combative. One clutch of gulls were allies. A few were loners, most were sociable but not particularly peaceful. We watched and watched. The warm rocks seemed to soften under me. I melted in the salty air, lulled by the creep of incoming tide swooshing and rattling the stones. My father and I kept up a relaxed querying. *What are they saying? What does it mean when this one does this and that one that? What is going on between those two?*

We didn't force conclusions. We just kept turning it over as data emerged. From time to time, if the gull action hit a lull, we conversed about something *other* than the gulls, usually something spurred by what we'd seen. Then we'd notice something new and be back to gull-focus. The water's edge slowly moved closer. A few gulls departed and didn't return. The group began to shrink, and we continued to watch. At one point, perhaps the sun went behind a cloud chilling the air, my father turned to me and said, "When is it time to stop watching?" and, both deciding that right then was the time, we stood and left.

That sweetest of days continues to enrich me not so much because of gulls, though they were brilliant, but because of everything—how my body savored the smells and breezes and temperatures, the companionship of my father, the birds' complex lives, and the posing of the true question, "When is it time to stop watching?" Maybe never. Asking that question was not meant to end anything. Instead it pointed at the nature of observation, which is a window into a slice of infinite continuum. A practice is that window—a time to sit or move and watch. What is going on? Watch what is emerging, turn it over and over, nab insights that then unspool. What we peer into is never finished. So we can relax, relax into our patience. In that fabric of patience is everything.

Invitation

How does our inner landscape open? Invitation. We invite what needs to be with us. We invite ourselves to move and to be moved, to explore and to be explored. We invite familiar pleasures and unknown adventure. They are not transactions—"I do this to get that." Since we are trained to do most everything as a bargain, only expending effort for a payback, letting this go may, at first, be tricky. It is enough to know that demanding a result—the transactional dynamic—gives us less, but I wouldn't worry too much about this heavy headset. When it comes to Invitation, our being hears the slightest whisper. One small piece of attention, one tiny gesture towards our centrality and the Creative Unfolding begins. Some days it arrives in a rush of light, like a long lost love standing at the door, delighted that we are home. Other days it is a faint glimmer. After a while, we come to trust this.

The Dancemeditations in this book are invitations. An invitation isn't a huge deal, and it works best if it is subtle. We simply shine the light of our awareness on a topic—our shoulder, our breathing, our skin touching the rug. Even the smallest shift from our familiar point of view—looking sideways instead of straight on, for instance, or standing here instead of there—proffers the invitation. We shine the light of our awareness and give it some time. This simple invitation to the self begins the melting journey. What is false melts. What is unnecessary melts. What wants to come can come.

Inclusiveness

On the mat, go inward with complete inclusiveness. Of course, we can't help but do this because we are each a singular, woven entity, but it helps to not live in the delusion that we can partition the self and seek wholeness at the same time. Take in the gnarly bits: pain, discomfort, fatigue, rage, depression, hopelessness, shame. Bring all the little notions authored by the constructed self, the shitty hecklers, the commentators giving poor advice, angry slave drivers, morose cynics, or indiscriminate admirers that have been allowed to run loose inside. Bring them without a plan, move, and experience your experience.

Open

I heard a lecture on van Leeuwenhoek, the father of microbiology who, in 16th century Delft, Holland, discovered microbes when he fashioned a rough prototype microscope to peer finely at the world around him. Neither scientist nor engineer, though he later came to be regarded as both, he was a draper who cultivated skill in lens-making to better see threads in linen. He was curious. Once he could see, he wanted to see more. He gathered drops of water from the nearby rivers, canals, and ponds that teemed with tiny life. No one had ever seen microbes. This accident of curiosity changed history. People could now observe a previously invisible world of creatures thriving inside and outside the human body, an ancient vitality defining Earth's living origins of which humans are mere newcomers. Our forays into consciousness are this story—the possibility of discovering what we don't yet know, what we cannot suspect, what is as yet invisible. This might alter our cultural mythologies. It will certainly reconfigure our teetering self constructions.

With regularity and sincerity in an inwarding way, the self we have constructed will lose its grip. We leave room for what we don't yet know, what even our cacophony of information—because we only look from the eyes we have constructed, rather than the eyes we could have—cannot encompass. How does this feel? The scent of the room, the air sliding along skin. Is it hot or cold? Is the ground hard or slippery or soft? Ahhh…my hand and arm seem to have their own way of moving to this music.

New may be subtle, easy to miss. It roams outside well-practiced organs of expectation until just now on the mat. Does it feels like regression, digression, unwinding, undoing, falling? Or perhaps rising, dispersing, coagulating? Maybe splintering, kaleidescoping, telescoping… billowing, exploding, submerging…These possible poems. Since we cannot *know*, we follow our yearning. Yearning is the lodestar as we leave the shipping channels for uncontrolled oceans. May we learn to love our yearning.

Don't Fret

Often we try to go in and can't get in. Don't worry. Don't fret. Be patient, keep going. During the period after two major surgeries to replace both of my hips, my regular hour on my mat was many things it had never been before. A bomb had gone off. I looked in and saw destruction and chaos. My inner bomb squad told me to get out, they had a lot of work to do. I withdrew. For two years, day after day, month after month, my stubborn mind checked in, saw the mess, suffered it, fussed with potions and therapies and mantras, and my body kept saying, "Go away. Do other things. Let us be." One day I lay on the floor with my knees bent, lower legs on the couch, and gazed in. The door was open. All was quiet. Orderly. The construction crew had finished, cleaned up, and departed. I wandered down dim corridors, through shadows and faint lights. Flashes of automatic movement so rare in my hips, nudged. Though I couldn't perceive the implants, the hips felt unequal. The left hip, the first to be replaced, loomed large with bulky scar tissue remnants from surgical maneuvers; no surgery is ever deft or subtle enough to leave a body as fluid and smooth as its native construction. The healing in the right hip lagged behind by two months. It appeared small and slender, its delicate presence marking its youth—a sapling, a steel sapling.

Last Night

I crawled into bed and the sheets felt like velvet.

These same cotton flannel sheets had, for weeks, been unhelpful bystanders while my skin popped and prickled with itches and pain as if rubbed raw. Despite a largely untroubled surface, my skin has been alarmed at every touch. No position, no clothing, no ambience could comfort me, though certainly a harsh wind, a hot blast, or prickly wool scarf was reliably uncomfortable. None of this was the skin I've known. The political discord of 2020 assaulted us, and my skin seemed to voice the worldly tension flowing through me no matter how I sought to comfort myself.

Then last night, before bed, I did an evening Dancemeditation with lots of friends on Zoom and the 'real deal' energy effervesced through me. We didn't focus on skin, but the foci were simple and singular and attenuated. We arrived in a quietude. I drew my drifting mind to the effervescence in my being. It blossomed. The energy worked in me and I was at peace. My skin finally calmed, even became capable of pleasure. When I climbed into bed, the sheets felt better than they actually are. Curled in the plant's boll I lay, breathing, the miraculousness in the puff of white on a stem whispering a lullaby to my skin.

This is no small thing.

Inner work is mysterious. I apply my steady self to soothing my frantic self. Calm down, calm down. With gentle effort, I draw myself to simplicity. Always this is the work. Though I want to control how I heal—fixing and doing—yet this assumes I actually know what's wrong. In truth, I rarely know the depth of difficulty in me. How many of us know the invisible nub of our cancer? It seems we are always looking inward as the 'aha!' slips deeper down just out of our grasp.

Over time, having practiced leaning on Succor, which comes to me with utmost generosity, I see that even when I know what's wrong I very likely won't know the cure. I won't know how to find comfort, but I can sink within and let the work do its work. The medicine and the healing. We can sink within and let the work do its work.

Comfort. Nothing is more precious, that feeling of safety and ease. It is so particular to each one of us, so intimate. These words are not about skin conditions and illnesses, but about how the depth of a meditation removed me from a collective anxiety that had been rendering my behavioral defenses porous and inadequate. During the meditation, I slid deep into myself. Submerged in True Self, the solace of an All-Seeing Beneficence delivered me into velvet. And so I slept well for the first time in weeks.

— Dunya, blog post

4 THE MOVEMENTS

My body dancing is an Ear to the Cosmos. If I stopped moving and dancing,
I would grow deaf and blind and senseless.
— Dunya

About the Movements

The movements matter, but not in the measuring that most quickly springs to mind with dance, namely appearance of whether the movement looks intriguing or alluring, or other visual performative criteria. Consider the antiphony, or perhaps antipathy, between ballet and Modern Dance. To the pioneers of early Modern Dance who were rebelling against ballet, the established dance form of the era, movements mattered. Early Modern Dancers devised their own movement systems. Doris Humphrey decided to extend her ankle but not point her toes. To Martha Graham, the human heartbeat was the core idea for her contraction and release technique. For Jose Limon, it was fall and rebound. Every choreographer sought not only to say their say, but to do so with movement mined from their body and experience. Modern Dance was an iconoclastic field of movement discovery and recodification—the wild, wild West of dance. Movement mattered.

Ballet, by contrast, has retained its limited set of movements—ballet steps—and ballet choreographers can't tinker much with these steps; they must make due by putting the steps in different orders, in different costumes, to different music, wringing as much as possible out of this material. In both these forms, movements matter, but in Modern Dance they matter just a bit more because the movements are less standardized. The movements demand precision. As well, because it is an instrument of design, the dancer's body must also be precise. Then we have athletics. Movement is precise, but as long as the swimmer is fastest across the pool, the appearance of the body is irrelevant. In athletics, movements matter and are precise in order to win the competition.

In meditation, movements matter but our criteria are wildly different. First, we aren't performing. It doesn't matter how we look. Second, we aren't competing. It doesn't matter how big, how fast, how strong, or how much 'more' we are than anyone else. The value of movements in meditation is neither visible nor measurable in scale. So what matters? Movements that are comfortable; movements that leave room to pay attention to a widening range of interior sensation; movements that focus less on execution and more on experience; movements that serve as springboards for interior life to expand and metamorphose.

Comfortable

First, comfortable—an imprecise, subjective measurement yet one that gives the sense of sensation. Let's imagine for untrained, moderately fit bodies comfortable implies an average range of motion—not 'the splits' and not a straight jacket—and an average amount of effort. For trained bodies, the range of motion and effort is wider. In any case, comfortable movement isn't too difficult to wear. No pants too tight for sitting, nor shoes too precarious for walking, nor voluminous skirts that catch fire and kill you. Neither do we want swamping robes of motion so amorphous they seem shapeless and give no purchase. Comfortable movement, therefor, fits easily within our body. Comfortable also implies feeling, and feeling good enough. The most useful movements, whether movement mantras or movement meditations, are not extreme and propitiate sensation.

Room to Work

Next, we want movements that require a moderate amount of attention. Since our journey is to expand and attenuate our ability to concentrate all our faculties, we need room to work inwardly. A Movement Mantra [caps???] gives us internal space to experience our component self—our sensation, our emotion, and our energy. We will tether our discursive thoughts to the movement mantra, and over the course of a movement period our mind will observe sensations, emotions, and energies that emerge and evolve.

Springboards

Springboards for metamorphosis. My criteria for this is vague. It involves a sense of the alchemical, the magical, and how can we be prescriptive about that? We just know we are heading that way and we use movement that somehow helps this happen. Can we tell from the apparent surface of the movement? Or is it in the sap? An an effluvium, or fragrance, or a flash caught in chinks? Perhaps we simply find a way of squeezing in between or, while still on the mat, falling off our perimeter.

Some Things that Did and Didn't Work

Being a professional dancer, I resisted giving up hard-won hyperbolic movement and attempted, at one point five years into my meditation training, to incorporate a few ballet steps into my daily meditation practice—*tendues*, *pliés*. I discovered that while my meditation skill deepened the connection to ballet, ballet did not deepen my meditation. On the contrary, ballet pulled me up to the surface of myself, initiating a self-criticism. This may have been bred into my training, and perhaps, had I persisted, it would have dissolved; or it could be a tendency inherent in the form's difficulty and idealism. In any case, ballet steps were not useful for meditation, but it was an interesting experiment. Belly dance, on the other hand, worked well because it is nature-based motion, is easy on the joints, and gets a lot of mileage out of standing on two feet on one spot, thus is excellent for moving with closed eyes. It began my rummage in nature-based movement.

Nature Motion

In early Earth eons, humans imitated creatures and natural geological forms to connect, to be like, to be infused with. One danced like the wolf to be inhabited by the spirit of the wolf. Asanas were named Cobra and

Locust and Scorpion because, like constellations, they resembled an animal's shape or way. Dervishes whirled in planetary motion. Dances were not decorative; they intersected and interrupted and interwove with existence, carried communication between humans, served as invocations in rites of passage, or as pleading to the heavens to send rain. Dances were essential components of original prayers. Then, as monotheisms made specious distinctions between spirit and matter, the body and its dancing language were downgraded. Swaying and pounding feet and gesticulation were pruned back and condemned. Prayer became mutterings in a kneeling body. The more civilized we have become, the more distant we've grown from the essential experience of movement as an intimate participation of self with Nature and with spirituality.

Before celestial observatories, we viewed movement with the naked eye and felt it. Now, our scope of vision is expanded. However it remains to those of us who journey inwardly to feel as acutely as the Hubble can see. Wonderment exists beyond our current capacity to measure. Movement that is either too minuscule or too vast for our current instruments, and movement that erupts and disappears before it is grasped, may be moving through our flesh, tapping us lightly, sharply, cracking our certainty until all we can do is lean into a Certitude we can't define or describe or defend to anyone, including our self.

Traditions and Discoveries

An illusion has grown up that we are different from the teacup, from the rabbit, from the puddle. I observe that most humans mistakenly perceive their moving body as a foreign object, separate from their mind with which they identify, and separate from all other existence. This thinking makes the body and its movement into something which the person doesn't know, doesn't want to know, or can't discover because somehow it is too alien. But here is the truth: every moving body inherently communes with environment, is shaped by the same physics of gravity, momentum, and thermodynamics, and is made of the same elemental material—carbon, oxygen, hydrogen. For me, in the most basic way, I work with movements that help me know that I belong, that I am, somehow, a different shape of the same things—the way ice, steam, and water are the same. The Dancemeditations are an invitation to submerge our way back to this ground.

Any number of movements—in fact millions of possible movements—

will work. Just as bioluminescent sea creatures in the Abyss produce their own light, the movements I have chosen to write about illuminate themselves from within, deepening and sweetening the more I attend to them. I didn't invent them; I have noticed them and caught them in both my cognitive and sensorial awareness; I have been gifted movement jewels from other dancers, animals, clouds, and oceans. In some cases, the movements I write about have been done as meditations for millennia by thousands of bodies before entering my body. They carry the seeking choices of preceding generations, and I am custodial to these precious messages.

I engage in meditations handed directly from teacher to student, vibrating with mysterious centuries-old transmission and enter a river reaching back, body by body. Though I move in my own immediate skin, experiencing the continual approach and falling away of my flesh and its motion, I also feel the beings that have moved in untold numbers of rooms, on every continent, clothed in cotton, wool, silk, linen, in shoes or barefooted, on wood or packed earth or stone or grass, under the same stars and different clouds. These meditations are at once venerable as Earth and as current as the breath you take right now.

I have chosen to write about a few of my favorites, but they are not the only possibilities. May many more emerge the way an endless variety of shapes burble in the waterfall. The Sufi way is a continual evolution stirring the ancient, the new, and the timeless into what is needed now.

5 BODY

In our burrowed and lidded darkness moves the mysteriousness of Mystery.
— Dunya

Ah, body. Let's go straight to the struggle which is 'loving the body.' It is rare to find a person who continually, unconditionally loves their body since body seems to happen to us largely beyond our control. Body is in control in birth, life, sickness, aging, death. Even those who enjoy their body off and on for a decade or two are disrupted when illness or injury or some other fleshly misfortune hits. As well as these inherent realities, most of us experience persistent physical dissonance because body represents enormous commerce in our lives: how much money we are paid, who loves us, if we are violated, which laws protect or fail to protect us, how unwritten customs utilize or abuse us. The gender and race equation; the fat, thin equation; the age equation. Body is the weapon of culture and in most cases, enculturation has stolen our body from us. It has stolen our ability to inhabit and know our body.

Body is how others see and treat us, and we internalize much of this letting how we are seen and treated determine how we see and treat ourself and how we make choices or endure choicelessness. Body becomes a whipping post when we feel powerless. We revile it when there is no other action to take. We heap blame on it for failing us. We are so utterly judged by physical appearance and capacity, and then beaten down by those judgements, that we must be forgiven for believing that this is what our body is. But this is not what our body is. These are interpretations, assigned meanings, and mostly, they are lies. I think resisting internalized lies is a hard way to oust the poison.

In this Path, we don't rewrite internalized scripts or pick at scraps of positives to outweigh heavy negatives. Instead, we experience our body ever more gently and deeply, and then we reach further in to fully experience our embodied experience. This ushers in love. We don't need to believe this or convince ourselves. We need only to let it emerge. The way to love our body is to feel, to be it, to know it from inside itself. As we progress in this embodied meditative Path, we come to apperceive that everything is body. Emotions. Dreams. Thoughts. Existence. Body is a continual poem.

In our Dancemeditations, we enter our closed-eyed depths and feel our way into what is most intimate, most secret, most initiating in us. To the origin. We do this not to avoid or transcend our body, but to meet it. We are ourself in our body. We are our body. The societal conditioning that harangues us in daily life and shapes impossible armor for our flesh, melts away. Sometimes slowly. Always inevitably. We inhabit our flesh deeply, experiencing our experience. Our body emerges from our innermost-ness until the wonderment within washes us into love. This is how we come to love our body.

I return once again to Bachelard's bird and look more deeply into this image. The idea of the bird and her nest has edges; she shapes her nest with her body. Unlike the bird our efforts are far more elastic and fluid and vaporous, and yet there is powerful shaping at work; our being shapes our body with its experience of itself. We sink into our innermost-ness, move there, dissolve there. Our experiences in motion change us. Without exception, this understanding, this experience, this animal, this divinity, this field out beyond, is true and fundamental, is wondrous, is love, is exquisite. Body is this. We reemerge into our ordinary waking world with this cellular glimmering which becomes our dominant experience of our body.

Our work is to find our innermost-ness, then trust this innermost-ness which moves within and throughout our cells to shape our flesh. Our work is to see that this continually happens. To notice. To participate. It is what we are. The love is in the body and is the body.

"I love this." "I love that." "I love you."
It is odd that we are possessive of love.
The truth is, a puppy or a tree or a person or a breath unlocks the garden gate
where love lives.
We open and enter the perfume, music, a sunny warmth, a fresh cleansing rain.
The love isn't ours. It doesn't begin or end with us.
We just suddenly notice where we are. We participate.
— Dunya

Part Two

FOUR Rs
The LARGER ARC

The process, progression, and scope
of a life-long embodied
meditation project

FOUR R'S: RELAXATION, RECEPTIVITY, RECIPROCITY, REST

Someone once came to their first Dancemeditation workshop on the strength of hearing these four words from a friend. They were intrigued by this poem and wanted to know more. In my usual fashion, I began wordlessly, leading movement with only an occasional verbal cue about breathing. I gave no introductory explanation. Soon we were side-by-side alone, sunk deeply in. At the end, I proffered the Four Rs—Relaxation, Receptivity, Reciprocity, Rest—as thumbnails to bag up and carry home the session's as-yet-inarticulable experiences—a little mnemonic to help our minds get a foothold after hours of nonverbal motion.

The Four Rs is a rubric of our somatic deepening into subtler and sheerer experience. It names an intentional, structured progression, and, in the Sufi way, is most often delivered at a session's conclusion to confirm experience. Perhaps because we immerse in these four conditions or states, I think of them as rooms in a mansion. We do things in each room, or are things, or do and are nothing. We enter the Hall of Relaxation, moving and breathing, feeling our bones toss in gravity's curving waves. Air eases into our nose and mouth, pushes open ribs and belly, then hastens out. We reach the Cavern of Receptivity. Arms, legs, lungs excavate tiny tunnels, burrowing down and down to somewhere ancient. A window sash flings wide to a mysterious vista. We billow into the Garden of Reciprocity. In the Realm of Rest, we nap, ringed in mist.

The process is generally the same because a process is a process, like growing up—first a childhood, followed by teen years, and so forth. You really can't skip over anything. However, as we journey farther into our depths and become increasingly familiar with inward journeying, we might wander back and forth between these rooms in the mansion of our being. It has taken me years to articulate these four simple words that are the heart of Dancemeditation. Relaxation, Receptivity. Reciprocity. Rest.

Most of the time we are in our own mansion. Then at some point—and this will be very clear—we are no longer in our personal mansion but have moved to a very different realm which feels a lot less like a room.

Sometimes
you have to
do the not doing
in order to
undo the overdoing

6 RELAXATION

All the little crannies yawned, stretched their stiff edges, saying 'come in, come in.'
— Dunya

Cutting Through the Crust

In the beginning, we literally and figuratively come home, put a key in the lock, swing open the door to Relaxation, a place where we dump burdens we've been carrying all day, or all week, or all our life, and close the door to outer pandemonium. We get down on the mat and move hypnotically, passing away from the clamoring street, though a quiet corridor, past a cloister with shadowed arches, and pause in an anteroom where we have time to collect ourselves. We breathe and bend, arc and torque and squeeze, lulling our controlling-ness to sleep; or move hypnotically and strongly allowing vigorous motion to release tension. On the mat, we practice the patient art of slowing, of feeling what we are doing, of noticing the sensation of breath, skin, organs, bones, space, gravity. We slow and notice and pause to digest what we are feeling. We experience our experience. Slow, notice, feel. I cannot say these words enough. The more we slow and notice and feel, the more we can notice and feel. Little by little, anxiety whittles down, and whispers of our real-ness sneak out to play inside us. Little by little, we cut through our crust of scars and fakery.

Constructed Self

Our crust. It's who we think we are, a personal identity we more or less consciously cobble together. We maneuver through the world using a self that we construct—ego, persona, astrological sign, enneagram type, and any other system of human definition—to deal with our day-to-day. We choose shoes, jackets, apples or pasta, homes, partners, religions, jobs, hobbies, pets. Are you a dog person or a cat person?

The word 'constructed' implies that we choose. Mostly we mold what is offered from the multiple choice menu of our time and place provided by our culture. Every culture has its ways and means; Western culture is all push and grasp, and those of us reared in it have learned to charge along deep grooves of consumption, aggression, and ambition in order to belong to our society. We internalize and obey these values. Our energy runs hot and fast into the grooves. We imagine we are okay until we aren't. Social conditioning is a sly, nimble thief inside our intimate body.

Certainly we need one another, and civilization is our attempt to manage togetherness, but in our hearts we know that to run and gorge is poisonous. We know we are being cruel to ourselves, to one another, and to the Earth. We give away our flesh, forfeit our potential, handing over self-sovereignty even before it is taken by illness and dying. Exhausting obedience is what we do until we get onto our mat and stop doing it, and Constructed Self is that capacious handbag into which we chuck the majority of what we will gradually be moving away from. We get onto the mat, close our eyes and move, go inward into extremely variable experience which calls and calls us and encompasses everything that the Constructed Self does not. We enter the Halls of Relaxation, the first room in the mansion of our being, and begin the slowing journey into the deep.

We amble along, fanning through a book, turning over a figurine, reacquainting ourself with neglected or forgotten bits of our past. They are part of who we are and where we've been. They belong at our banquet table of self-awareness. We invite all of who and what we are, get to know them, the motion, emotion, and sensation all mixing, scattering, flashing, streaming, in streaks, bursts, and stabs, one triggering another. We cannot predict what has snagged on a particular movement, or area of movement, or texture or timing or force, because when we were in trouble in the past and had to get through a situation or endure difficulty without a lot of options, we stuffed the trouble somewhere—maybe in our brain's back bedroom, maybe in our gut, maybe in a lung, or baby finger.

On the mat, this could happen: "Every time I turn my head to the right I feel teary and scared" or "I get woozy in my stomach and want to yawn and sleep." To manage painful emotions, we have clamped down, gone numb, overreacted, spaced out, and now as we relax, these unpleasantnesses bubble up. Learning to relax isn't so easy nor should we expect it to be. On a thick Persian carpet in the quiet anteroom we move and breathe and feel what we are doing. We rock our crying, hungry infant self. "Hush for a moment."

The negative unravels as we weave the positive.

Do the Not Doing in Order to Undo the Overdoing

We need to do not doing in order to undo overdoing. This is what we don't do even as urgent impulses rise: Need to check my phone. Need to eat something...again. Need to pee. Need to wash the dishes, call so-and-so, buy a new whatever. We don't do them. We do the not doing. Not doing is its own work, inaction an action. We are not doing our habituation. We are not doing our escape hatches. We are not doing our running away. We are not doing our self-destruction. We are not doing our self-starvation. We are not doing our self-flagellation. We are not doing our do-goodness, not doing our self-righteousness, not doing our manipulation, justification, pain, despair.

We are not doing all that. We are not rehearsing our Constructed Self. We do the not-doing, and it undoes our overdoing. Street dust falls off our shoulder. Our hot feet cool. In this pause, what is the sensation of not doing? Is it disjunct, a bit absent, or like the breath got punched out? Maybe an upwelling sluices over, or nothingness, or chaos. We are full of breathing and body sensation and time and space and the shape of a room and the weight of our limbs. Not doing feels different. To not jump up and run isn't nearly as much effort as our typical over-worked slave-ways, yet it is unfamiliar.

Fortunately, we aren't doing nothing as we do the not-doing. We move and breathe and feel, disengaging our ticks and drives, slipping out of the groove, a sort of sleight-of-hand in the body. Our practices are deceptively playful and unostentatious because if we tell ourselves to be serious and fix this, then we are just practicing self-correcting and perfectionism and competitiveness. Cajoling ourselves out of our

Constructed Self is the trickiest aspect of our sojourn in the Hall of Relaxation. A friend once said, "Dancemeditation is such a pleasant way to do what is difficult. All this dancing around, all this beautiful motion. It looks innocent and trivial, but we are flying in shadows to slay our dragons." We do not-doing, undo overdoing and finally notice that something else is going on, has been going on unbeknownst all this time.

Finding the Moment

One summer I stopped because I was forced to stop, stop, stop, stop in all possible tracks for longer than I had ever stopped. I had had surgery and needed to recover. I had permission, from all the world and from myself, to rest, to mend. It had quite an effect on me. I stopped feeling that I ought to do anything else. My body turned to my dense, crammed, stunned head and shook her, made her notice the moments, the Moment. I sat quietly observing a frenzied world, people zipping here and there, maniacally contributing, desperately doing good, trying to control the world, and artfully sidestepping chasms yawning right where a foot was about to step. We hate to fall. Even more, we hate to be falling, but we will. Something, someone, somehow will rip away our ground, and grasping does not stop this.

As I gradually emerged from an invalid condition, instead of feeling comforted by a return to normality, I hesitated. Who am I now? I wanted to get going again but felt uneasy, dissonant, knowing I couldn't walk backwards. I had stopped. I had changed. I had broken a momentum, and it didn't immediately feel good. I inched my way forward confused and lost, and to make this long story short, on the other side—because there was an other side a few more months of healing down the road—I poked my head out of the fog into clarity and authenticity of self, less cluttered by cultural programming. I was energized. But something more important had occurred. I knew, without a doubt, though I have always known it—and we always know it because when we are in it, it is unmistakable—the Moment is the place to choose, to go, to explore. And the Moment is easy to whiz by.

The Moment

The Moment. The lacuna between one breath and another. Losing track of time, time stopping, timelessness, that easy "I've got all the time in the world" feeling. We know this sweetness. Finding the Moment can be like cruising along the highway and seeing signs for the Grand Canyon."Gotta get there," We push down the gas pedal, drive fast, scanning, rushing. Got to get there. After a stretch, the signs are gone. Somehow we missed it, missed the Grand Canyon! Because it doesn't stick up. It is down in, an enormous cleft in the Earth. That's how peace is, how the Moment is. Without learning to relax, slow down, notice, we zip right by.

It's there. We have to learn how to recognize it. In the beginning, as a result of our excruciating patience (for which we might feel extra virtuous) or with blinding speed (for which we might feel special), we are rewarded with the beautiful magic of the Moment. The Grand Canyon. We have chosen to go to it and found it. Then it is gone. It is maddeningly slippery journey, but if we keep choosing and going and noticing, we will know it is there and we will know how to find it.

Here is the hard truth: as long as we are nervous, as long as we feed and occupy anxiety, as long as we distract and clutter, as long as we are not in the Hall of Relaxation, we will not be in the Moment. We will not feel peace. We won't know timelessness. We will not be present. There are no exceptions. There is no way around this.

7 RECEPTIVITY

Receptivity is the shimmering pivot in consciousness work. Receptivity is the motherlode.
— Dunya

A Different Sort of Ecstasy

We move toward the murmurings we've heard from within and arrive at a pleasant reception room, the Parlor of Receptivity. "Come in. Come in!" Our Host greets us. "Dance is a doorway in, not out." We are received. We will receive. Inwarding, onward we go, in visual darkness with closed eyes, leaving behind the confines of our Constructed Self. The Host regales us with stories and listens to our tales. One door opens to another, each deeper in than the previous. We begin to forget who we thought we were. Now we dance, and we aren't making it up, expressing to others, or even aware of others. Not a show and tell, not what others think or have to say, not about pleasing them. Notions of dance and movement and our body as entertainments for others dissolve. *Dance is a doorway in, not out.*

With our gaze turned in, we feel the soft touch of the Host drawing us forth. Our Constructed Self gives way to our Being. We receive and absorb. Nourishment is not only food and human love. We need what is in air and space and dreams and beauty and mystery and possibility just as surely as we need a meal and a roof. We need what we can't see— magnetism, momentum, resonance, ineffable palpability. Though we can't fully understand this, we know this. We know, when touched and immersed by it, that the Invisible is essential not only to a fulfilled life but to the most basic life.

Now, we feel our way like a blindfolded baby, then like a mole with tiny feet and tremulous whiskers, then like a starfish, its under-limb cups sucking and releasing in slow fluidity. Submerged in bodily interiority, we sense our existence. Tap, tap, slide, a warm whiff, nubble or silkiness or the glassy smooth, thrums and chords and breathing, a hiss of clothing, airiness. Back in the other world, words separate our capacities into strata—interoception, proprioception, intuition—but in the Rooms of Receptivity we inward our way as a whole creature within our deep animal humanity. Our body is not what we imagine. Not an envelope separating the numinous from the manifest.

Embodied Dreamscape

In Receptivity, we inhabit an awake, embodied dreamscape. We enter our cellular presence. We are incarnated. We stop galloping out beyond and sink deeply into our true fullness. The illusionary identification with transcendent thoughts ceases. Just because we can think does not mean we exist beyond that which allows us to think. Thought is body and body is thought. Thought is a very thin yet powerful substance with a sensation of burning in our craniums, yet it is sourced from belly, breast, skin, toes, the churning of the microbes we host, and the trajectories of our solar system pulling our elasticity.

The thoughts we contrive are the tiniest zephyr of these massive forces. In the innermost rooms, our most intimate spaces, an ever-modulating, ever-morphing, invisible ambience fills us. We are washed wide open. We fall in love with our breath. Aeons run in our blood. Our flesh becomes a cosmic ear, our motion a listening. We swim in wonderment, and wonderment swims in us. Our heart opens its glistening eye and inner vision—*basira*—awakens. This sweetness is an unusual flavor of ecstasy. As linguist and theologian, Michael Sells, distinguishes so beautifully in his book, *Early Islamic Mysticism*, this ecstasy is not the *ek stasis* from the Latinate root of 'standing outside of oneself, out of our body,' nor a rapture, the *raptus* of 'being taken or 'seized up out of oneself,' rather the Sufi ecstasy—*wajad*—is an intensity of finding within, an infinite inwarding, as well as inwarding into infinity.

Pivot

On the mat we have been downshifting, focusing on sensation, re-orienting our attention and awareness, occupying our thoughts with something other than their usual folderol. As thought subsides, sensation brightens. Sensation is a very immediate beast. It is about right now. We are cold right now. We are too hot right now. We are comfortable or energized or sitting or standing or driving or tasting the banana right now. We are on our mat right now, bending forward and exhaling right now, and now coming up, inhaling. Our minds have been loosening, sentences turning into phrases, phrases into words, and words dissolving. We have not yet disappeared, but we've been losing track of thought, of pattern, of personality shape, of linearity, of causality. As sensation increases, rationality subsides. As sensation increases, time-tracking dissolves. As sensation increases, presentness increases. We alter not only the content and density of mind but the way it engages. Our mind, rather than leading, begins to watch and follow. This is the turning point in consciousness work. The pivot.

Following-ness in the Ocean of Dark Space

How does this pivot happen? In a way it naturally emerges as we slow and notice, and yet there is particular mechanism which helps because, if we merely disengage habituation, we can just as easily reengage with it. When I first began to study meditation, I followed my teacher. He taught by moving slowly, meditatively, as we followed. Wordless learning was new for me. I initially thought he employed this method because he wasn't fluent in English. Over time, I understood that he spoke English plenty well enough to teach with words but chose not to, and I experienced how the lack of words helped my mind quiet down quickly. As well, it was clear that a spiritual fluid or cloud or substance with no name filled us all as we followed him. Following is rich with gifts. We see, feel, and absorb with our whole body. Pick it up. Catch it. Use all of ourself.

'Follow' is a cousin to 'receive.' Following is how we awaken and entrain 'following-ness.' A group gathers. A teacher leads, and the groups follows. After, the group forms a circle with one person in the center, and the group follows this Leader; or in a circle of three or four, the Leader role passes around the perimeter from one to the next; or in a twosome, partners alternate roles. (Some call this 'mirroring' but a mirror is glossy, rigid, flat. It breaks and brings bad luck, or the shard cuts us. It demands our perfection. We are yanked to our eyes out of the chewy juice of belly and thighs. It is a fine flashy word but too loaded for our soft creaturely bodies.) The Leader closes the eyes and moves intuitively. The others follow, receiving the Leader's movement. Though no one is touching, the Leader's unique quirks, pacing, grace or awkwardness sink directly into the others. Body to body. Felt and unfettered. Body ingesting body. We know the sensation of another's flesh and being, what is similar, what is different. We feel, receive and absorb. In this nonverbal interchange, the Leading is 'speaking' and Following 'listening.'

We follow another person's motion, feeling something we've never felt before, and our mind finally relaxes and quiets. It doesn't have to analyze or invent. It doesn't have to keep up. A horse carries a rider. No one, not even the person leading, has to think of what to do because—and this is the key learning in Lead & Follow—even the Leader is following. The Leader follows the movement welling up from inside their own body or passing through their body. The Leader is listening. The depth of the Leader's dive allows the group to also go in. The purer the leading, the sweeter the following. In Lead & Follow, we awaken and entrain following-ness.

Now we close our eyes, enter our own world and follow. Follow what? Follow our body. Follow sensation. Follow sensoriality free of thought girdles. We might be surprised at how easily movement comes up. The music plays. We move in an ocean of dark space, and suddenly our spine and limbs, feet and hands, belly and back are swaying and tapping, and darting and swooping and surging. In the time before birth, in our mother's inland sea of pulses and beats, we danced, and our body remembers, has been waiting for something like that liquid dark. It can be this easy. Just a matter of letting it happen. We can stop assuming that because we aren't thinking of what to do that nothing will happen. Something will happen, if given a chance.

In following-ness, our body moves its truth, and our mind listens and treasures our flesh. We receive and absorb ever more deeply from an ever more deeply moving Truth. In comes a deep breath, softening our shoulders. Our feet hang heavy into ground. A shaft of sun is an apron on our lap. We are in the new and new. We grow familiar with newness and relax our grip on nameable destinations. The word 'explore' suffices. Receptivity is the shimmering pivot in consciousness work.

Receptivity is Asking Deeply

A dancer, Sufi friend told me a dream in which she was performing a perfect ballet arabesque, the sort of movement only a few people in the world can do. Her voice trembled with surprise and pain and joy as she related waking and knowing that ballet had never been her dream; ballet had been her mother's dream for her as well as her mother's dream of having a daughter who performed ballet. For my friend, dance—not ballet —was her calling; yet for much of her life her mother's dream had been inside, pushing her, confusing her.

Her story is probably a story many of us know. We carry dreams within that are not our own. It is not easy to let go of someone else's dream and to know our own dream. Dreams can be trickier to relinquish than pain because we naturally want to alleviate our pain. Living the wrong dream is more difficult to see. Dreams are alluring, bobbing and glittering in front of us, full of promise and pleasure. However, a dream that is not our own, not from our own true nature and true calling, will eventually disappoint. We won't feel right. We won't feel without doubt. It may break our heart.

Finding our calling is a life-long project, leading us step by step, closer and closer to a place without doubt, and unless we are heading there, we won't feel cohesive and consonant. Sufis call this Certitude. Our calling— why we came to this Earth at this time—may not be dreamlike and pretty, but it feels clean and true. In Receptivity we ask deeply, not from our head but from our totality. We let our mind follow our body, our body follow the great flow, our being receive and the waters of Truth wash in.

One More Time—The Moment

We go towards the Moment as quickly and directly as possible. Stop preparing; stop doing this and that to get ready. Just go. There are no prerequisites, only the direct trajectory into the center—the straight path, which is not a moral directive nor a set of strategies. We need only know where we are heading and trust the process of the Four Rs. Move sincerely towards the Moment and the Moment will come toward us.

We can never know how the Moment will be coming toward us. And then, somehow, we are There. The Moment is the ocean, the brine of tears and tides all around. It is the little oceans of salty water in every cell. The Moment is inside and out.

Sheer

The music played. My body felt easy and even. In a while, movement so tiny I barely knew it had begun was here and there and everywhere. All through me, music moved my body, and my body had a lovely time. I didn't have to dance. She danced for me. So sweet. In a dark sanctum, inner raptures weren't in the shape of swells and cadences, or ocean waves, earthquakes, or blades of light. They were more akin to the fragrance of rose, to a lingering echo in a vast cathedral, the ubiquitous magic living in in-between spaces. That sheerness is there when I let go of all that I create and simply receive.

— Dunya, blog post

8 RECIPROCITY

We opened our heart's gaze to the great firmament.
We were standing in the garden, in the fragrance of roses, the Host
everywhere and nowhere,
Our flesh everything and nothing.
There was no day, no night, no come nor go, no time, no turn.
— Dunya

Fruit of our Labor

Reciprocity is a nonordinary state. Until now we have been aware that we are a self working with a self. In Relaxation, we drew our focus to movement mantras, opening to embodiment, exploring and immersing ourself in an unfolding that was no longer muscled and willful. The crust cracked. In Receptivity, we pivoted toward deep asking and nourishment. Inside our concentration, inside the sensorial focus and mental focus, inside following-ness, we softened, mutated, and let go. Yet all the while we knew we were a consciousness doing an effort. In Reciprocity we enter the fruit of our labor, a sustained and sustainable pulsing, generating more energy than we use, in fact rolling in a momentum beyond an oscillatory equation. We moved beyond the limits of our imagination. Reciprocity's holism, while still relaxing and still receptive, tastes of limitless infinity. Beyond the Beyond. Within the Within. Beneath the Beneath. Between the Betweens.

Palpability of Nonordinary States

Within deeper and deeper inwardness, experiencing greater and greater subtlety, we become sheer filament and membrane. Though less in overt sensibilities and sensations, we are not out of our body. Instead, unstuck, what we never knew we could be swoops like a flock of birds, connected and harmonious, miraculously expanding and contracting in the trees and wind, singing and then quiet, in the large tide of what is. In it, we belong, yet 'we' aren't there. Oscillatory condition passes. Integrated into creation, absorbed in the moment, our interior strata flow, feet speaking to legs, stomach to hair, belly to breathing, vision to hackles, our cells to the room, to the Sun, to Andromeda.

For all humans, reaching this gently undulating terrain is a place of newness. We have never been just here before. We have never really been without our 'I-ness' or our 'my-ness', alive and awake in purity of Being. The Sufis call this *hal*—'an unprecedented, unique state.' We recognize a waterfall though the falling water infinitely changes. That is *hal*—recognizable yet ever-changing. Our capacity to inhabit the nonordinary states of Reciprocity is fitful at first. They are strong but temporary. We continue to practice, and subtly, gradually the states come more frequently, and the periods in the first two phases of our process are shorter and easier. The non-ordinary states become dimensional as worlds, as realms. The realms are, and 'we' aren't. Through the repetition of states and the growing ability to sustain them, absorbing and renewing and connecting and receiving, we shift. An ocean of Truth wears down our small rubble. Reciprocity leads us to waking inside our life. We are in communion with 'what is,' alive in this cosmos. Here is the miracle of multiplicity and vibrant, ineffable joy. We are essential, elemental, eternally creative, which is the nature of our universe, this continual inventing, recombining, chemical motion. This is incomprehensible but palpable.

Reciprocity is the engine of genuine embodiment. Our journey is always experiential, always palpable no matter how subtle that palpability is. We must feel it. What is our body? This question cries louder and louder the more subtly we penetrate. Once we begin to know our bones as spacers and our cells and microbiome as collaborators, we have to question outdated, erroneous models of body and of spirit. Are they hierarchic? No. Are they separate? No. But how do they flow and what are they and what are we? Where do we really begin and end in every sense of individualistic identification? Our skin, our breath, our ideas are not the edges we imagined. Reciprocity erases our perceptual separateness, without relinquishing our embodied sense of being and the palpability of experience. There is nothing quite as ecstatic as the Subtle. The sheer sensation of flesh liberated into its Truth. Vibrant. Attuned. A tendril faintly quivering in eternal song. Our body, though apparently a discreet containment, is our envelope of numinous knowing, our dissolution into Nothing and into All. In Arabic, the word for this beautiful Unity is *Tawhid*.

9 REST

When in deepest peace, deepest beauty.
When in deepest beauty, most divine.
When in divinity, deepest peace.
— Dunya

Ah, lovely Rest! We rarely give Rest proper respect—it's that thing we do when we are not being productive—yet without it we would exist bound up and wound up, our experience of our experience only half experienced, our breath only half breathed, and sensation only half felt. Without rest, we would survive in diminishment. After Relaxation, Receptivity, Reciprocity, we arrive at Rest, right? No. Rest is not an end point. Rest is the warp to the weft of actions and non-actions in Relaxation, Receptivity, Reciprocity.

One thought I dearly love is that need for rest is more fundamental than our brain. Researchers at Kyushu University in Japan identified a sleep-like state in a tiny, freshwater animal called a hydra, which has a simple anatomy and lacks a brain. "We have strong evidence that animals must have acquired the need to sleep before acquiring a brain," said Taichi Q. Itoh, the study's lead author.

Rest is existential. Rest is the weaver of our moving tensegrity. An ocean wave surges then recedes. Sound waves have peaks and valleys.

Our movement surges and pauses, intensifies then subsides. The antiphony of heartbeat and breath oscillate between effort and rest. Wave form underpins all we do and are.

Forms of Rest

Sleep—often the deepest form of rest—is mysterious. For most humans, it is hard-wired into daily rhythm. It comes over us, eclipses our day. We aren't gone or dead or vacant; we are alive, breathing, percolating. Our systems purr in their quiet, sustaining repairs: heart beat, blood flow, spinal fluid coursing up and down, breathing oxygen in and detritus out. Our nails grow, our hair grows. Our brains pop with current and chemistry. Relentless thoughts may pause, but dreams and visions bleed and blossom. Rest is rich.

Rest is not only sleeping. (Some people sleep and never rest—they have forgotten how to unwind or even that they might need to unwind.) Rest is not only being stretched supine gazing up at drifting clouds, not only being still and quiet with eyes closed. Rest is also moving and dancing and walking without demanding that we be different than we are in this moment, in this room, in this flesh, now. We move and let go, noodling, doodling, at ease. Existence and consciousness is not a puzzle to piece together, not a problem to fix. If we've been trained to feel everything wrong around is our mess to clean up, or even possibly our fault, and therefore that 'living is fixing,' we might momentarily panic at the idea of vague, nonproductive experience. The terror of being selfish and lazy. What crazy inner labor! We cannot make the world be or do anything. As poet David Whyte puts it, "To rest is to fall back, literally or figuratively from outer targets, not even to a sense of inner accomplishment or an imagined state of attained stillness...." We can rest in stillness, in sleep, and in motion but always when we stop maneuvering and demanding and controlling and forcing and correcting. Add your own words here that capture the exact flavor of your personal trek into exhaustion.

In Rest, nothing has to fit just so. The edges needn't meet, or colors blend. It can be peculiar and outside the norm. It can be so so so subtle. It can be a one off. In learning to rest, we learn to trust what is not that slave master in us. We learn to trust our body. Let the self sort in its own way, body sort on its own. Trust and Rest seem very close to one another.

Ways of Lying Down

One way of inhabiting Rest is to stop moving and lie down, either prone (belly down) or supine (back down.) We close our eyes. We Rest. There is no other cue to focus on, perhaps just a gentle awareness of body sensation or breathing. It is fine to fall asleep or let thoughts ramble or amble off. The time is there to simply be at ease. Sometimes, after moving and relaxing in our motion, we lie down to Rest but lose our condition of Relaxation. Lying down triggers anxiety. Did we leave the stove on? Is the dog in? Does our lower back begin to ache and the floor feel obdurate? Do we feel vulnerable? Lying down itself can be uneasy for all kinds of reasons and what appears restful can be pocked with discomfort. A simple focus can help. Lie down, close our eyes, and feel our breathing and the sensation of our limbs' weight, bringing awareness to the physical experience of the pause. This is steadying. It helps suspend mental discursiveness, tethers a mind that has difficulty settling, and soothes inner shots of anxiety. And now, patience. Breathing and feeling our flesh. Breathing, bit-by-bit letting go into gravity, letting gravity cradle us. We are safe here.

Resting in Motion

Another way of inhabiting Rest is to drop our attentive focus and continue to move freely, letting our mind relax and wander; in fact, letting our mind unwind or space out while we continue to move. Relaxation and Receptivity cultivate restful, dynamic embodiment, being in our flesh without pushing and grasping and forcing, without responding to compulsions and anxiety, without constantly obeying hidden internal agendas. For instance, rather than accommodating a body dysmorphia that urges us to move prettily even when it feels unpleasant, we could instead explore ways of moving that feel satisfying without regard to how it might appear to others. When we turn away from stressful patterns, our jumpy flesh calms, which in turn makes our experience of our body and psyche more restful. We breathe more slowly and fully which makes breathing more restful. Our embodiment becomes a more restful home, a more restful habitation, a more restful incarnation.

Word Pairs: Excavate, Integrate and Ingest, Digest

I like these words pairs emphasizing the value of rest. To draw attention to a particular focus and stay there while inner fractiousness unwinds requires effort. Then let go of effort. Rest is a period without attentive focus, whether moving freely or sitting or lying down, to savor the fruiting.

Excavate and Integrate belong to solitary meditation. We close our eyes, focus on one idea, and burrow into its dimension, thus the notion of excavation. We might tether our attention to our bones, or forehead, or on circular lines of movement—there are a million possibilities—using the topic as pic and shovel to mine our body's treasure. Concentration is an effort, and we continue to concentrate even when we feel uneasy, or mentally weary, or when nausea whispers at the edges. Not only is it work to stay on task, but we are as well, not reacting to the little nudges of anxiety. I always love the Sufi term for these nudges—*nafs*. It is like having a little homunculus yanking on our shirttails, poking us or worse, nipping us like mosquitoes. *Nafs* are our inner mosquitoes. Not giving these distractions our life force but staying on our little task is huge effort, though quiet and unseen. Integration happens when we release focus and let our body move as it wishes. We float and flow while self turns over and sorts its discoveries—the glittering gold and rough rocks, our stoney layers of petrified forest, strange leaves, and primordial creatures. We don't have to oversee this part. Our work was in the digging. Moving freely after attentive effort is a form of rest. We are resting in motion.

Ingest and Digest belong to interpersonal practice in small or large groups or with a partner. When we follow another person as they do their own dance, our body ingests unfamiliar ways of moving as well as the presence in a body that is not ours. Our body also ingests the 'feel' of that person; our body takes in what is not us. We might do a twenty minute period of Ingestion. To then 'digest' this intake of another's motion, we close our eyes and let our body move how it feels, resting in motion. Or we might lie down and rest.

Stimulation

I wrote the following when taking care of my father following his stroke. His situation was desperate, but it showed me that all humans, even in health, need a balanced antiphony between stimulation and de-stimulation, which is another way of saying effort and rest.

> *Folding: He folds and unfolds a blanket. He asks me to help remove his medium blue pullover wool sweater. Right away he wants it back on again. Then off, then on, again and again. Though the activity at first entertains him, I see that this isn't about comfort; it is perseveration—the repetition of an action with no particular aim, like a loop. It is a fugue state common to dementia. He is uncomfortable no doubt, but this dressing and undressing have no effect on that discomfort and soon these repetitions will devolve into agitation. The actions overstimulate his delicate nervous system.*
> — Dunya, journal entry

My father's actions seem extreme, but they are no different from how we all are. Watching and helping him, I saw in stark relief behavior I had observed in myself and others all my life. We launch into fruitless patterns, fall into addiction or depression or mania, tangle in frenzied actions. We cannot see any more than he could. In retreat settings, we rest more, de-stimulate more than typical daily life allows. Those little rests when we lie down after an exercise and the music plays softly, or there is silence, is de-stimulation for our nervous systems. That simple. Less stimulation. Less input. Rest.

The Reach of Rest

There is a place we reach—some of us, sometimes—where self has dissolved. 'I' is annihilated. Awareness is all that is. Lightness, freedom from self. It could be death. It could be a living innermost-ness. Like taking off a heavy mantle and running free, this is also Rest.

> *I come into the presence of still water.*
> *And I feel above me the day-blind stars*
> *waiting for their light. For a time*
> *I rest in the grace of the world, and am free.*
> — Wendell Berry

10 THE LARGER ARC

As for constriction and expansion, their mode of consciousness occurs in the present moment.
— Qushayri, 11th century Persian Sufi

When we could no longer meet in person during the plague year of Coronavirus, I conducted twice-weekly Dancemeditation sessions live online going month by month with a periodic month off. The group, which soon felt like a community, was wonderfully consistent. Though not formalized, it seemed as if we were at Dancemeditation College on an extended course, and this regular, building accumulation of practice brought a larger arc of development into play. One afternoon, before an evening session three quarters of the way through the year, a heavy drawing inward exhaustion overtook me. At the same time, I received texts and emails from several others in the group saying they also felt exhausted. "Ah," I thought. "Here it is again."

This portentous mood, the herald of a spiritual oscillation mapped in the Sufi mystical tradition known as Contraction (or Constriction) and Expansion, has always been part of extended trainings since the beginning of my Sufi study with Adnan and thereafter during my own in-person retreats. I continue to appreciate that Sufi has terminology for this arc of experience some of which is difficult and tiring and inscrutable, and some of which is creative and joyous and delightful.

Contraction and Expansion rests at the heart of Sufi psychology, and often the experience is like being held in an enormous heart-like fist that energetically squeezes then slowly releases the seeker. Theologian and scholar, Michael Sells, writes in his masterful book of translation and commentary *Early Islamic Mysticism*, "Constriction is the gripping of the heart, an experience analogous to fear, but far more intense in that it is an experiencer of something immediate, in the present. Expansion is a dilation, a feeling of peace or well-being, again intensified down into the immediate present."

Contraction and Expansion, spoken of as a singular motion, for one does not come without the other, emerges from beyond one's will and willfulness. The seeker shifts at a deep, organic, difficult-to-pinpoint level of self as a result of *himma*—spiritual longing—and persevering practice. One's seeking has set this shift in motion and once it begins, no matter what you attempt, you cannot go back; you cannot extricate yourself. Though difficult to understand and uncomfortable to experience, it helps to know that this is how we change. This is us growing. By comparison, insight and cognitive tracking are minor. The words Contraction and Expansion, translated from the Arabic *Qabd* and *Bast*, are a bit curt and dusty, insensitive to an experience that pulsates and quivers with vibrant inscrutability, so I sometimes use the words Deepening and Flowering.

The Deepening

In the early days of a retreat or extended training, we open subtle internal channels neuroscience and medicine have not yet mapped. We go in, over and over, as far and for as long and with as much attention as we can muster. We are unrelenting. We are dogged. We burn off trivia. The familiar entertainments of self look tiny and childish. A sense of infinite energy grows. A wild tornado-like sonorousness roars in our scaffolding. We tremble. We are near to bursting. Our devils whine at the perimeter. We weep. But so what? Those feelings are distant slipping sparks. Sprawled on a vast ocean floor in profound sleep, restless exhaustion roams our bones.

Everything we do makes our skin feel tight, yet we walk with even steps to wash our hands and drink our tea, and our meditation clothes rest elegantly on us. We have gotten used to the others practicing alongside us, but not to this self. We are growing infants in the too-tight womb ready to be born. We are in our Deepening.

At last in some moments, we breathe untorn. A long narrow footpath has been winding us through thickets, sometimes steep, other times vertiginous and crumbling. It is not always dramatic. It can be monotonous. And now, though we don't know how this has come about, we are free, circling Earth, looking in and out from its iron core, north and south, east and west spreading in our blood. Time uncoils. We could stay here forever. We have no qualms and no argument. This is the sweetest sweet, the Deepening.

The Flowering

Later...sometimes days or months later...we begin to flower. We are fresh, rinsed, washed in hard-to-reach spots. The prison door is open, or it is gone, and we can't remember its suffocating color. We feel vital, creative. Our truth is not a muffled murmur but a clear aria singing through our day. This is the Flowering. Eventually, we might live here, and if not quite yet, at least we know it exists and we know how to go there.

— Dunya, blog post

I think it helps to know that Contraction, which began with the heaviness I mention above—and yours might feel very different—means we are moving toward our heart's desire. The 12th century Sufi Master Junayd said, "We have been liberated in eternity from the bondage of things." Strong words, but when we work in nonordinary seeking, the changes that occur are equally nonordinary. A century earlier, Persian mystic Qushayri, whose *Treatise* is the most popular classical work on sufism, admired for its subtlety, acuity and clarity, said of the seeker being saturated with energy, "The expression used by some: 'I am full,' that is, there is no room left in me." We might not understand what is happening anymore that we can see the totality of a storm as it crashes around our house. After, in due time, there is an Expansion.

One Flowering

The retreat is over. Everyone has just left. I stop. I felt an enormous stillness. I am alone in the quiet desert.

After a while, I gather myself to move about on my own time, breathing as I scour the fridge, breathing as I bin up the remaining dry goods. It is too soon to assess the retreat or understand internal motions. I need to lie down and sleep, and I will in a little bit, but just now I hover in a billowing.

Past the Wash Yard, where the red pump stands still after two weeks of squeaking up water for campers, tiptops of piñon and juniper dance beneath the overspreading blue. A delicious taste of autumn threads the breeze. I set out across the meadow toward a fragment of distant rim peeking through an aperture in the trees. I know that tonight a coyote close by—it will be right outside the window— will give out a long, thin, ghostly howl that sinks to a warble then the tiniest, single yip. A moment later will come a distant response—the antiphon of wild things. I know this, though it hasn't yet occurred, because I am in the All Time.

— Dunya, Journal Entry

If They Only Knew

*What earth is this
so in want of you
they rise up on high
to seek you in heaven?*

*Look at them staring
at you
right before their eyes,
unseeing, unseeing, blind.*

*I was patient,
but can the heart
be patient
of its heart?*

*My spirit and yours
blend together
whether we are near one another
or far away.*

*I am you,
you,
my being,
end of my desire.*

*The most intimate of secret thoughts
enveloped
and fixed along the horizon
in folds of light.*

How? The "how" is known
along the outside,
while the interior of the beyond
to and for the heart of being.

Creatures perish
in the darkened
blind of quest,
knowing intimations.

Guessing and dreaming
they pursue the real,
faces turned toward the sky
whispering secrets to the heavens.

While the Source remains among them
in every turn of time
abiding in their every condition
every instant.

Never without the Source, they
not for the blink of an eye—
if only they knew!
nor the Source for a moment without them.

— attributed to al-Hallaj, 10th century Persian mystic; Michael
Sells, translator

Part Three
DANCEMEDITATIONS

Movement meditations
and thoughts about them

TURN AWAY, TURN TOWARD

Is our body a portal or a portcullis? The words share the French root *porte* meaning 'door'—yet one fences us out while the other sweeps us in. For many years I have practiced the Sufi Whirling. The Whirling is a continuous turning on one spot for 30 minutes. It is a beautiful example of movement mantra, a repetition moving into a singularity. For years, I experienced Whirling as a seamless singular motion until one day I saw that because we have a front to our body with seeing eyes and a back without eyes, I was also continually turning away and turning toward. Such a simple but profound perception. We turn away, we turn toward. Conversely, when we turn toward, we turn away. It had the sense of choosing, a choosing built into our body and thus quietly into our lives. We choose without knowing that we are choosing. A bird flies up to a branch away from the ground. It is natural.

In these Dancemeditations, we turn away from the external and turn toward the internal, away from disembodiment and toward embodiment. Rather than working out, we work in. We turn away from feeling incapable, diminished, overwrought, fragmented, disconnected, and toward trust in our body's language, dreams, information, and intuition. We turn toward awareness of breathing and motion. We turn toward the sensation of skin and bone and fascia. We turn toward an intimacy with self. We turn toward Mystery and Communion and Belonging.

Oh, keep squeezing drops of the sun from
your prayers and work and music
and from your companion's beautiful
laughter, and from the most insignificant
movements of your own holy body.
— Hafiz, 14th century Persian poet

SECTION ONE: MOVEMENT MANTRA

DANCEMEDITATIONS FOR DIVING DEEP

11 MOVEMENT MANTRA: REPETITION, EVOLUTION, & MOMENTUM

Repetition simplifies. Repetition gives us time to feel. Repetition settles us into our ground. Repetition is hypnotic.
— Dunya

Repetition

The word 'meditation' conjures time swept clean of overwhelming complexity and avalanches of obligation and thought. The broom? Repeating one simple thing. The focus could be breathing, or swaying side-to-side chanting a prayer, or moving in wave-like repetitions with simple stretches or circular flows. For the following movement meditations, I borrow the term 'mantra'—Movement Mantra. Movement Mantra shares territory with its better known cousin, sound mantra. In sound mantra, one repeats a sacred or numinous phrase. The words have meaning. As well, the actual sound of the words has sonic resonance. The repeated phrase itself doesn't change; at the end of the hour practitioners are still incanting *Om Mani Padme Hum.* Similarly, Movement Mantra is a movement topic with salubrious or sacred qualities that have physical, universal, or natural resonance—turning, rocking, wave, vibration. In Movement Mantra, the topic, like a mantra, stays the same for the duration as the movements themselves gradually evolve, gently shifting over the half hour or hour of meditation.

Here is a significant difference between sound mantra and movement mantra. In sound mantra, the syllables have meaning, a perceived or assigned significance. The topics in Movement Mantra are important, but before discussing *what* we are repeating, let's look at the nature of repetition itself. Both movement and repetition are pre-verbal. Our creaturely nervous system has been moving and repeating long before the advent of language and meaning. Thus when we do movement mantra, we descend beneath language and language-type meaning to an elemental strata of self.

What Happens As We Repeat

Repetition gives us time to experience our experience. Repetition simplifies our existence for the moment. We reduce stimulation. We have time to notice what we are doing, and we don't have to notice a million things, but only one simple thing. *One thing at a time. Simply breathe, lifting and lowering one hand, over and over. Just that. Less stimulation. Less complexity.* As we repeat, feeling the sensation of the movement, we can note where we are inside ourself and where we are in the room. After while we settle into what David Whyte terms 'the ground of self.' We can come down from being overwhelmed and overstimulated. We get over our jumpiness. We calm down. If we are doing gentle movement—like rocking or swaying—we are soothed, and if, on the other end of the spectrum, we do vigorous repetitions, the movements stimulate our circulatory system and diffuse pent up anxiety.

Repetition is hypnotic, lulling our discursive, distracted mind. In technical terms, repetition initiates a downshift in brainwave patterns from Beta to Alpha and Theta. Repetition balances brain hemispheric activity. Repetition activates our parasympathetic nervous system, one of three divisions of the autonomic nervous system, sometimes called the rest and digest system. The parasympathetic system slows the heart rate, increases intestinal and gland activity, and peristaltic motion. In other words, repetition initiates quieting embodiment. Even without a salubrious significance, repetition itself is powerful.

Untangling Meaning

Repetition creates meaning and destroys it. We learn our human life, for good and bad and every shade in between, through repetition. In meditation, we unlearn through repetition. The first happens consciously and unconsciously; the second only happens consciously. On our mat, we close our eyes, inhale reaching out one arm, and exhale pulling it back. (That's a good Movement Mantra—inhale with one movement and exhale with another.) If we have never put attention on the sensation of reaching out and pulling back, we have no sense of its place in the firmament of self. Skin brushing against our clothes, bones sliding inside tissues, moods triggered like a scurry of mice—all these have been happening in us yet are as unknown as if happening to someone else. We have been unaware and so our reaching out and pulling back has had no meaning. Now we notice, and just as waves endlessly roll, grinding rocks to pebbles and pebbles to sand, we erode our ingrained identity.

We keep going. We repeat. We observe. We feel. We notice. Waves over rocks. As we grow conscious of reaching out one arm and pulling back, we feel the movement. It becomes weighty and meaty, not that faint disembodiment of our typical ways. Soon there is the flutter of forgotten birds nestled in our flesh. A pastiche of fragmented narrative and sensorial blooms that taste of revisitation seep through newly emerging awareness. Reaching out and pulling back excavate in the murk. The movement is a melange of past and present. We repeat, we observe, we feel, we notice. Waves over pebbles. We sink into an abyss of formless space and unmetered time where design draws itself through us. Rather than rehearsing or creating who we are, we discover what is there.

We repeat, observe, feel, notice. After a while the old meanings dilute and empty of drama. We arrive in a fundamental tide, a sea of electrical charge, a dimension outside imagination's limits where we perceive our movement's ever–changing interior nature. Without the detritus of our past clinging to it, reaching out and pulling back is a fresh miracle of itself. Knowing more about our movement evokes the paradox of knowing nothing at all. The movement is not a wilderness of unknown, nor a desert of too-well-known, but a cultivated garden of non-definition.

Repetition and Evolution

The more you repeat, the less it stays the same.

If you could lift and lower your arms exactly the same way for an hour that would be fine, but it is unlikely, and unnecessary. Repeated motion incrementally, continually morphs. It may intensify or accelerate or grow dense, gradually change its direction, swing wider and wider until the originating movement devolves, even loses cohesion. Our movement may evolve because our muscles get tired; or the message in the motion wears down its edges; or the movement evolves not from fatigue but from opening from inside its intelligence; or from receptivity within us, or from without. Close attention to repetition inevitably leads to the movement evolving on its own. Which is what we want.

At times in our practice, we begin with a simple movement, like bringing our arms forward as we inhale and back in as we exhale. We stay with this movement for a while until we sense that we need to change. We then change one small detail—for instance, our arms lift a few inches higher than before; or sometimes we do another movement that is similar, perhaps the arms going to the side rather than to the front. The changes are moderate, but we stay with the topic of connecting our breathing with our movement. We continue gently, as if we don't want to disturb the baby inside us that is drowsing down into sleep. We want our entire being to slow down, calm down, settle down. We want to wind our way in. The repetition and the small evolutionary changes de-stimulate our nervous system. We do this as a conscious, active process.

At other times in our practice, repetition lulls us quickly into inner quietude, and we receptively observe our movement evolve or devolve without cue or cause, the energy of the repetitions having their own momentum. We watch. Repetitions gather or subside on their own. The repetitions roll downhill, fall away, and vaporize, particles drifting apart as magnetism ceases to adhere the shape. Or the movements cantor then gallop then compress into flights of their own, borrowing our body, spinning our fatigue into vitality from within the motion's own wisdom. This we ride. A pendulum in gravity. A rolling snowball. Mist dissolving into sky.

Momentum

A body is mostly motion, a roller coaster from one piece of space to another.
Motion peers through curtains of fascia, down halls of skin, pries apart pores, and
breathes out to join wind, river, cloud, sea.
  — Dunya

Momentum is a science-y way to name what mystics call the Moment. *Momentum is what happens when we are moving in the Moment.* In my early dance years, I felt like Dorothy in the 'Wizard of Oz,' moving and dancing, circling me around the heart of the matter, yet locked out. I wanted to go home, wanted to be in that effervescent hypnosis I'd felt when gazing into the waves curling at the bow of my father's sailboat, but I didn't know how. With the Sufi work, I went right in, and I learned how to always head my dance there. One certain dynamic was that of momentum.

Momentum is the key attribute of Reciprocity. Moving *into* the state is an effort, while being in the state is effortless. No longer grasped by friction or gravity's heavy draw, our action powers itself. Our body-being has located its spatial coordinates, oriented its mass to ambient magnetism and now, bit by bit, releases extraneous effort. We are stable. We are carried in the curve. We are carried in the swoop, in the arc, in the turn, in the Whirl. Movement Mantra moves us from Receptivity into Reciprocity.

12 MOVEMENT MANTRA: BREATH DANCES

Move to your breathing—the rhythm, the gush, the stutter, the sigh.
— Dunya

The Taste of Breathing

Breath is the body's commerce, its wheeling & dealing, whirring & stirring between inner & outer space. Breathing comes in many flavors, shapes, and timbres. Deep and slow, rhythmic, musical, strong, elongated, suspended, thin, thick, sucked in like syrup, or whispered in like silk. Some breaths are breathed silently and stealthily, others sonorously. And then there is air. We have all breathed in exhaust fumes, cooking scent, garden perfume, sweet cut grass, odiferous farming manure, stinky urban toilets, pungent sweat. Sun-baked rocks dry our nostrils. The pine forest's cool damp moistens them. Coffee. Hyacinths. Ocean. Every inhale carts particles into our lungs, and every exhale spews bits of us out into space. I have my favorite air as do you. I also have my favorite breaths.

For most people, favorite breaths are long and full and slow. Lungs seem to open indefinitely, the alveoli unfurling like peony petals. There's no rush. Our body tingles in the rich bath of oxygen. One person might envision the color of their breaths as red and red and red and magenta and carnelian and crimson and carnadine and fuchsia and wine. All the blood shades and their cousins. Maybe someone else perceives breathing as silver or gray. Every breath carries a world of knowledge. What portrait of a place slid into your nostrils the day you stood in that dry, bleak back room or in the dank basement? I'm not asking about what your eyes saw and tacked to your inner gallery wall. I mean what touchable world lived in the inhale you took to stay alive, that you now take every few seconds to live?

One thing is certain: Our breaths save us. (Our breaths are always saving us from death.) Our Central Nervous System regulates environmental rigor, yanking oxygen out of hidden bodily stores and dumping carbon dioxide, keeping arterial blood red and veinous blood blue. Structural Integration specialist, Mary Bond, says of breathing, "There is no one correct way to breathe." This offers us liberation from the urge to control. Though we needn't make one way right and another wrong, neither does it infer stuffing breath awareness into the closet of unconsciousness. In Dancemeditation, breathing instigates, inspires, and supports dancing. It is also its own kind of dancing as variable as any other kind of movement.

Vernacular Breathing and Meditation Breathing

Runners pant in concert with the slap, slap of their feet—an even, rhythmic in, out, in, out. With swimming, the breath cycle is disproportionate: the in-breath is a gulp and the out-breath elongated, spanning several strokes. It is the same for singing. Quick inhale, then sing out and out and out. Some talkers chat nonstop, and you wonder when they inhale amidst all those exhaled words? The other day I took a walk with a friend. We trudged up a long hill pushing our pulmonary limits, the huffing and puffing altering the cadence of our conversation. This sort of breathing—what I call vernacular breathing—supports activity.

Then we come to meditation where breathing is the topic. In meditation, breathing is neither random nor natural. Breathing practices are specific, variable, nuanced, honed. Breathing isn't harnessed to make us better at an activity. From this foremost perspective, we unfold all other self-observation. In meditation, breathing is the fundamental ground. The meditation breathing with which we are most familiar is *zazen*. Sit crosslegged, the spine upright, hands in a particular position, eyes closed or barely open with an unfocused gaze, and breathe. Sometimes the instruction is simply, " Be aware of your breathing." Sometimes the instruction is more detailed: "Focus on the in-breath" or

"Concentrate on the in-breath passing through the gate of your nostrils."
There are many subtle variants. 'Be aware', 'focus', and 'concentrate'
suggest varying shades of effort. For me, 'be aware' is wide and gentle
while 'concentrate' feels dense and singular. The physical stillness of *zazen*
makes breathing easier to locate and perceive. In my experience, sitting
still and watching my breathing, or more particularly, watching the
procession of in-breaths entering the nostril gates, encourages my
respiration to unfurl its wide wings like an eagle rising into the sky, as if
the watching has liberated breathing's beauty. I draw attention to my
body's relentless bellows, awestruck by breathing's magnificence.

In Dancemeditation—I just say this again because it's important
—*breathing instigates, inspires, and supports dancing. It is also its own kind of
dancing as variable as any other kind of movement.* We move with closed
eyes. What we perceive with our inner gaze is complex. Muscles, nerves,
bones, joints, arteries, veins, capillaries, fluids, organs, fascia, and dermis
shift everywhere simultaneously in every motion. Music courses through
us. Efforts and lines of motion burst forth and slide away. What do we
attend to? The mind skitters. The instruction of exactly what movement
to focus on can range from the specific to the permissive. In Breath
Dances, the verbal cue—that is, the suggested Movement Mantra—
invariably includes attention on the breath. It could be something like,
"Be aware of what you are doing. Be aware of your breathing." Or " Let
your body move however it wants. Be aware of your breathing." And so
forth. There are thousands of cues, each worthy of years of practice. Our
breathing becomes more prominent as we dance more deeply in.
Breathing, either as leitmotif or as centrality, disassembles the mind's
choo-choo train obsessiveness. We are at first disparate pieces of action—
movement, breathing, feeling, not thinking—reaching towards one
another. In a while, we fall into the middle of the whole motion.

Breath Dances of Dancemeditation

The Breath Dances of Dancemeditation cleave our movement's pace to
repetitions of breath cycles. The tempo ranges from rapid, to moderate,
to slow and elongated. We sit or stand on our mat, eyes are closed. Strains
of measured or unmeasured music fill our auditory field. We exhale,
bending forward for four beats, then inhale and rise back up for four
beats. The spine's curl and uncurl slowly press air from the spongey lungs
then let it rush back in. The symmetry of the breathing is determined by

the symmetry of the motion, and both the tempo and the symmetry of the motion are determined by the tempo and symmetry of the music. As we observe our breathing, it grows more elegant, less raggedy. Breathing slips its unruliness into this glove of restraint, and if, at first, the chemical exchange in our blood makes this uncomfortable or even unattainable, at length we settle in. What we recognize as self—pulses, gushes, thoughts, spasms, impulses—loses its jive and jerk. Our brain waves' vertiginous peaks and valleys subside, growing long and shallow. There we are—our brain in another state. The mind trails the body's steady walk through the forest of time, the last to notice what has happened in the blood river touched by the lung bellows and the sway of the willow spine. Thought swings in and out of the movement and breath, catching a sense of our embodied poetry. Thoughts become bits of gold thread in the fabric of breathing.

Of course it isn't just our brain that has changed; our entire biochemistry has shifted. Attentive breath-woven motion navigates us from an unconsciousness fraught with cortisol and alpha waves into a lagoon of beta, theta, omega with its lush lapping of endorphin, serotonin, and dopamine. Mystics through the centuries have called these by other names—elixir, the jewel in the heart, the secret rose garden. The message, however, is the same: movement and breathing carry us from one world to another.

Slow Breath Dance Meditation
Meditation: Begin sitting or standing in a comfortable neutral posture. Find your breathing. When you are ready, inhale with one movement and exhale with the next. Repeat the same movement pattern for a while as you become aware of moving and breathing. Use simple gentle movements, like lifting the arms on the inhale and bringing them down on the exhale. As you continue, allow yourself to linger in time. Your breath can elongate and your movement slow. Over time, as you relax, you'll feel an organic evolution in the progression of your movement patterns. Continue with this for a while. Afterwards, let your body move as it wishes.
Eventually, lie down and rest.

Do movements that are easy, that are gentle. This is not for expanding muscular reach. Instead, we use movements that we feel lightly, and, as our attention clarifies, we feel and notice more and more of the entire motion rather than the end points. For example, we might turn our head to one side on the inhale then back to center on the exhale and so forth. Rather than aiming for the farthest part of the turn in order to feel a strong stretch in our neck, we attenuate the motion to better feel the entire act of turning. Slowing depends on the pace our breathing can manage. The idea here is not to force the process, but to aim patiently, gently towards slowing.

Her Breath

She let her breath sink oily and heavy into the bottom of her pelvis, then drew it up, hand-over-hand, along the center of her body. It made its quiet way into her head where it spread, tickling the inside of her skull. Her breath touched its tendrils gingerly along this membrane, fine veiny lines of sensation, filaments or root hairs.

Her breath seeped out, drained down her neck and throat as if drinking itself. It whooshed along the tube of middle-ness into a deeper, dimmer space behind the stomach, behind the fat, slick ropes and globs of guts, the shady underbrush of organs. She swam through snaky reeds following her exhale that was emptier than common everyday breaths. It reached into a basement of itself. Empty. Beyond the urge to suck in.

She lay fallow. Hollow, dry. Then, she lifted the gate a tad, let air ease in, like a secret, like an Unknown. It drew her embers from beneath ashes, took the tiny heat curled in her tailbone, tugged and tugged, as if digging up a resisting root and swelled with sudden freedom upward, the warmth billowing on a rise of air.

Up the center, up and up the column, up into the winged lungs that fluttered, happy about breath returning sweetened with dark earth and volcanic fire, thick with organ murmur. Breath scattered into alveoli like puppies running on the heath. The chest, from front to back, shouted, "Hello!", a trumpet of sensation echoing from rim to rim. Finally came a fluting through the throat. Fine notes, swollen with oxygen.

This was a true breath, a felt breath, not a mechanism, but a poem; not survival, but a flourishing. Breath delights in this castle, she knew, in the ornaments, the halls of splendor, the trick wall in the library that opens to a dark back corridor. She followed that story, the spiraling stone stairs.

We were breathing there together last night, laughing, trembling, turned in on

ourselves. It was an uncountable place, unspeakable. I was lost for a long time. I
loved it. I'll love it again.
— Dunya, blog post

Rhythmic Breath Dance Meditation

Meditation: Find rhythmic music. Drumming is wonderful, something that isn't hectic, frantic, or Olympian, preferably generated by human drummers' hands and arms rather than electronic beat tracks. Close your eyes. Settle into the swell and fall of your breathing. After a while, include the sound in your awareness, letting the rhythm seep into you. Now let the pace of your natural breathing meet the the pulse of the drumming at any tempo—fast, medium, or slow, your breath landing on the beats. Stay with this for a while. When you are ready, begin to move, your movement emerging from your rhythmic breathing. Don't force your body. The breath and motion are carried in the rock of the rhythm. Your outer eyes are closed. With your inner gaze, observe what you are doing—your body, your organs, your body's motion, images in your flesh, whatever is there. Let it flow by without getting caught. As you continue, let pulse and breath direct your movement, movement taking on a life of its own, finding its own momentum. Continue to bring your breath and rhythm to the forefront of your awareness. Continue for at least ten minutes; longer if you wish.

After a while, relax your focus and let your body move however it feels. Afterwards, lie down and rest.

Slow Fluid Stretching Meditation

Meditation: Begin sitting or standing in a comfortable neutral posture. Find your breathing. When you are ready, inhale with one movement and exhale with the next. Repeat the same movement pattern for a while as you become aware of moving and breathing. For example, you could bend forward over your legs with the exhale, and come back up with the inhale, repeating this again and again. In a while, when you are ready, shift to another repeating movement, perhaps bending side with the exhale and coming back with the inhale. Continue with this new repeated pattern. After a while, go on to another. See if you can feel when the movement itself wants to shift. As you continue, settle into the methodical flow of motion, the movements elastic and

stretchy. Over time, as you relax, you'll feel an organic evolution in the progression of your movement patterns. Continue with this for a while. Afterwards, let your body move as it wishes.
Eventually, lie down and rest.

Go with what your body needs. Some days it needs restful stretching, and other days it needs more exaggerated elongation. The personality of this practice is wave-like, oscillatory, evolutionary. Each wave of a repeated motion shifts slightly as we accommodate the softening timbre of muscle tone. And sometimes there is little or no repetition. Just stay with breath focus and go with what the body needs. As we relax, our flesh rewards us with its native inventiveness. We don't have to think of what to do; our body has so many things to show us. It wants to explore. Our main participation is as witness rather than manipulator or fixer.

One Day Out of Thousands with Slow Fluid Stretching Meditation

Breathing & Bending Forward, 1998

I bend forward sitting crossed legged. I expect to feel tight, but I don't. I feel springy. This is heartening. I continue on, breathing and slowly bending forward and coming up. Each time brings another perception. I try small subtle variations of the bend; how I time my breath, observing where the breath flows within my torso as muscles and organs contract, how vertebrae shift in relation to one another. Sometimes my pelvis leads and thorax follows. Sometimes the whole bends as one unit. After a while, my hips want to move. I stretch my legs forward into a new world of sensation, the backs of my legs like long bright wires. I gently run my hands along my outer calves and over ankles until fingers splay across the tops of my feet. Inhaling, I suck gently back, hands sliding up over my knees. Slow. Tidal. The way waves creep up the beach and suck into the belly of the Bay. The backs of my thighs resting against the floor fade back. They release their awareness of intensity. Soon, I fold flat against my thighs on the forward bend. I stop there and rest, my stomach pulsing gently against my legs, the way my dog used to feel under my feet at the dinner table in winter. She slept there as we ate. I took off my shoes and warmed my feet on her belly. Her sleeping breath soothing me, protecting me against the world of intellect that surged around my head above the table—food, talking, anxiety. Under my feet, under the table, in the dark was peace.

A depth emerges now. My brains swells, thickens inside my dark skull. My closed eyes gaze backwards into my squishy tissues and also gaze forward into the outer edges of a vast space. I return through this to crossed legs. I bend softly side, my neck streaking into perception. My body is a nest of fairies glimpsed at the edge of twilight. I slip through a chink into whispery sensation. I have put down my savage ways.

I inhale as I come up from the side bend. Exhale as go down. I feel loving of an odd sort. A new way. New for today. My upper back shifts, muscle sliding over shoulder blade, so well-oiled, so sensuous. Every day it does this. Every day I have a miracle of sensuality inside myself. Everyday my body makes love to different parts of itself, muscle to bone, fascia to organ. They lean and whisper love to one another, my breath their music.

I peel my body out of space and ladle my back onto the floor. Everything pumps, the cacophony of pulses and breath and fluids and lymph. My energy swings up and down and around inside my frame. My breath gradually sinks down and opens. I sigh deeply. My ribs are free. I subside. So much has happened, is happening. I am beyond thought again, resting now. Floating. Air settles on my skin and hair, creeps under my clothes, enters my nose. I feel how Earth is miles of lovely heavy air leaning on our bodies. I feel how different it is to live on Earth than anywhere else. Though I have no comparison, I feel it anyway. I have been breathing. It is not mechanical. It is poetic, full of shades of meaning, songs of my world in every coming and going. One Sufi said, "Our lives are one long sequence of breathing practice."

— Dunya, blog post

Natural Breath Dance Meditation

Meditation: Choose medium tempo music that is repetitive and non-intrusive. Sitting or standing, close your eyes and let yourself quiet down. Now bring your attention to your breathing. What is it doing? Let your body begin to move however it wishes while maintaining your focus on your breath. The breath and the movement may not coincide or obviously emanate from one another. Let each go their own organic, comfortable way as you observe. What is unfolding in your breathing? in your movement? Stay with this for twenty minutes. Your attention may come and go. That is fine. Keep bringing yourself back to what you are doing. It will be interesting to note correspondences, or lack of, between the breath and motion.

Afterwards, either lie down and let your mind rest, or let you mind relax as you move in any way that feels right at the moment.

After a while, rest.

Taksim Breath Dance Meditation

Meditation: Close your eyes and feel the sensation of living. The breath coming and going, its hush inside the ear. The ground pressing the underside of the foot. Air resting on your cheek. Viscera curled like sleeping bears. Now come back to your breathing. Without grabbing the air, let it come in when it wants to visit us. Later on, let it leave. A good soundtrack might be a windy day in the forest, or Persian or Arabic taksim. The music needn't mesh with the breath. Let the music influence breathing. Let the music, and the presence in the inner and outer worlds 'influence' rather than 'adhere' or direct you. Suspend, linger, dwindle, textures unfurling outside the sense of drive. Take your time. Whenever you are ready, let your body move from this breathing. After a while, let the movement subside. Rest.

Where I was raised on Cape Cod, wind is continually stirring trees into sighing rustle and the ocean into lapping and crashing. There are steady winds of course, but I am thinking of the more common blustery days with surges and pauses that resemble breathing. The sky breathes music into the land. Wind is the Earth breathing. Indoors, I grew up hearing Western music which is predominately metered. Then, along the way, I met Eastern music. Middle Eastern *taksim* opened a living, ancient world. A solo musician winds and stretches a discursive melody into long sweeps of surge and ululation. Expansive. Peaceful. Spacious. Arrhythmic. Free from drumming and without a metered nature, this music is ripe with timelessness. Moving inside Arabic or Person *taksim* or Indian raga, slows one's movements or, more precisely, encourages one's movements to slow. Our breath can discover its own natural pace. We may, with noticing, discovered that our breathing not only elongates its methodical, measured breaths, but its unmetered breaths as well. Breathing is capable of arrhythmic non-pattern.

13 MOVEMENT MANTRA: ROCKING & ROLLING

Our Universe wiggles and waves and, as we rock and roll, we resonate with the elemental.
— Dunya

Rocking

My friend, who works in hospital memory care wing, remarked with a sigh that we used to have rocking chairs to soothe the elders. Now we use medication and restraints. What happened to rocking chairs—and not just for old folks? Today, houses are littered with recliners and loungers, but as a child I remember a rocker in every living room. A mother nestled her infant against her breast and rocked. The baby slept on a breathy rise and fall to the steady thrum of her heartbeat. People rocked on the porch or beside a fireplace, chatting away worldly troubles. Rocking chairs calmed those in the grips of dementia as the sun set. If a person couldn't run or walk long distances, or trim the hedge, or mow the lawn, they could rock and knit, or smoke a pipe, or sip a cordial. People tipped back and pitched forward. Their fluids sloshed. The length of their frame rippled with small sequential movements. Gravity rolled beneath haunches. Their spine undulated ever so slightly. The visible periphery slipped and slid. Rocking in rocking chairs, hammocks, and swings, was part of comforting in domestic life. Rocking was—and still is—a peaceful, constant, ever-shifting repetition. Rocking Meditations gently loosen a tight body. After session of extended Rocking, we rouse and sit up, relaxed, wide-eyed, and slow. Rocking brings us safely home. Rocking is deep medicine.

A rocking chair rocks because we push with our feet, or pump our arms, or some wonderful person pushes us. Rocking Meditations employ the same principle. A body part—arm, hip, foot, side of a leg—acts as a propellor while the rest of the body relaxes, unwinds, and unfreezes.

Pelvic Rock Meditation

Meditation: Choose some easy-going, rhythmic music. Lie on your back with legs extended and close your eyes. Find your breathing. Let your body melt into gravity's embrace. When you are ready, center your attention on your pelvis. Let your legs relax fully. Begin to rock your pelvis. Don't worry about the direction—side-to-side, up and down—but strive to initiate the rocking from your spine rather than hip sockets. You may need to remind your thighs —which tend to grab and push—to let go. Let your buttocks turn to jelly, thus not lifting your hips away from the floor. Release your neck and shoulders. Release your jaw. As you continue, the motion will find its own pace and way and may not always coincide with the music. Let the rhythm of your rocking interplay with the music's rhythm. Let the Rocking 's dimension and tempo naturally evolve. Continue to subside into gravity, releasing unnecessary effort. After a while, let the movement wind down and cease.

As you rest, feel how you feel.

Sternum Rock Meditation

Meditation: Lie on your back with your legs extended and eyes closed. Find your breathing. Release any tension, and let your body sink into gravity's embrace. When you are ready, draw your attention first to your sternum, then to the area behind the sternum between your shoulder blades which rests on the floor. This area between your sternum and the floor, called the mediastinum, houses your heart. Rock your whole body from the mediastinum. As your upper back pushes against the floor, feel it widen, soften, grow warm. Continue on, the rocking finding its own evolving pace. Release unnecessary effort in legs, pelvis, neck, jaw.

In a while, let the movement wind down and cease.
As you rest, feel how you feel.

Heel Rock Meditation

Meditation: The Heel Rock activates occipital release and balances spinal fluid rhythm. Recline on your back with your legs extended. Close your eyes and find your breathing. Let your body sink into gravity. Notice where your heels rest on the floor and notice the top of your metatarsals as they face upwards into space away from the ground. Keeping the heels where they are, gently move the metatarsals toward then away from your head in a small motion, as if your feet are waving to someone in the distance beyond them. If you are relatively relaxed, this tiny motion will rock your body, your skull and pelvis tipping up and down as if nodding in agreement. Skull and pelvis ride along with, but don't initiate, the rocking movement. Don't worry if this complimentary action doesn't immediately happen. Keep going for a bit, relaxing as you wave your metatarsals. After while you will feel body release. Continue to settle into gravity.

In a while, let the movement wind down and cease.
As you rest, feel how you feel.

Hypnotizing Our Body

I first developed Rocking Meditations as a soft mesmerization, particularly helpful in the midst of extended retreat when participants needed periods of quiet expansion. Over time, Rocking revealed healing and deepening properties. I include only three specific meditations here; there are many more, but the idea is that one part is the motor while everything else relaxes. I encourage you to unearth your own because this motion may be small, but it is mighty.

Rocking Meditations, like most Dancemeditations, hypnotize our *body*. Which is quite different from lulling the mind. If we lull the body the mind will follow; the opposite is not necessarily true. Life fills us with protective reactions. As we rock, our defensive reflexes diminish; our nervous system jettisons extraneous effort; the propelling body part encounters less resistance and labors less; the entire motion becomes more efficient. Though it may take some time, our body will unwind. This is the observable somatic shift.

Our physiological processes attenuate as well. This following roster of benefits is my expert opinion derived from my own extensive experience and from conversations with massage therapists, bodyworkers, medical professionals, neuroscientists, and trauma therapists who have participated in my workshops and experienced these meditations. As yet, there is no definitive clinical research.

Here is what we all believe is happening. By activating the Parasympathetic Nervous System, Rocking encourages a more restful, recuperative physiological state with a slower heart rate, lower blood pressure, and increased peristaltic action. Rocking stimulates our lymphatic system, which protects us from infection. The pace of blood flow and spinal fluid flow harmonize with the rocking rhythm and allow our system to stabilize. Rocking supports our endocrine system, which regulates tissue growth, body temperature, heart rate, blood pressure, cortisol balance, energy production (glucose/insulin), and pain control (endorphin). Rocking purrs along in a smooth sea, casting its calming spell.

When we rock lying down—these are the meditations given here—our frame sinks toward the ground, our bodyweight pressing the soft tissue of resting body surface into the floor. The rocking motion becomes a massage. The gentle kneading squeezes our spongey interstitium, hydrating that connective tissue. Rocking's soft rhythmic pressure against the floor—like using a rolling pin or Pilates roller—helps gently dissolve built up fascial layers and soften scar tissue. About scar tissue: we injure a shoulder, and, because it hurts, we don't move. Our body bandages the injured area with layers of gauzy fascia. Immobilization helps torn shoulder fibers mend, however, without movement, this scar capsule grows dense and hard. Then, because our nervous system memorizes a limited movement pattern, we forget to move the shoulder, and our range of movement remains diminished. Scar tissue can be dissolved, and rocking or rolling is one method.

Last but not least, here is how our muscular system likely benefits. Certainly Rocking softens muscle bundles, yet I am most strongly drawn by this subtler idea: Rocking is gentle and can whisper into shadowy corners we can't reach through overt efforts. Let's consider our muscular habit of freezing our movement out of fear. Rocking murmurs to our frightened body that we are safe. Now our nano realms let go. This is true for both traumatic incident and for insistent daily stresses. Hectic, overwhelmed lives are mentally and emotionally distressing, but they also invite a defensive somatic responses. We brace in small, continual ways, initiating body-wide tightening. As our body's tiny diverse motions diminish, the once juicy webs of fascia begin to stick to one another and grow chunky. (Just like the description of scar tissue above.) We don't ripple and flow. We move more woodenly, have more pain, are fatigued because our movement is laden with resistance. We contract. We freeze. It is possible that the stiffness of old age isn't only a slowing of circulation. Perhaps it is also the result of a lifetime of bracing and never melting. We rarely recognize this significant tension. We've grow accustomed to it, yet it is a prison. I think it is unrealistic to expect that an occasional massage or periodic vacation can unwind the insistence of daily tension. For our modern plight, regular doses in a rocking chair or of recumbent Rocking Meditation seem like a sensible restorative.

For all the technical material above, I come back once again to the prime directive: we dance to resonate with the elemental. Our Universe wiggles and waves, thus it is no mystery that Rocking moves seamlessly into a mystical realm. For me, part of mysticism is mystery. I am unfailingly surprised how doing one simple thing offers an unexpected and beloved experience.

I Thought Rocking was My Mother

One evening...

...I stopped rocking and was effervescent, like water swirled in a glass then set on the table where tiny bubbles rise in waves carrying light-filled air to the surface. In stillness, my spine felt prehistoric, an animal that had existed before Earth made imprints in rock layers, an animal untraced, except for vestiges left in my body. This animal lived in an Earthly world, slow and in the habit of watching. It craned a carapace spangled with eyes toward a gravitational field that sprouted unknown plants. My face was rubbery, melting, a false thing. My head fell back, thunk, decapitated, and my neck opened into a dark well out of which nothing could climb.

I lie on the ground, my rocking rib cage an ancient bark floating its cargo over the wide, restless sea. I lie on the ground, my rocking rib cage a basket cradling my organs, those little babies nested and safe. Safe. So safe.

I rocked on and on. My heart grew lively, wanting to jump up, wanting to laugh and run away. And why shouldn't it be that free? It could be that free. My heart has had to be stalwart and steady, keeping the body going day and night, slowing then quickening, never stopping for long. I've been too much that way—the solid girl, always stalwart, never getting up, laughing, running away.

"How I want to banish your cares, soothe your pain so you can be free, but I'm too small for that odyssey, so we sink together to the bottom of the ocean, into a dark world, stirring in the rockweed, in a sea change into something rich and strange, my Father." I thought rocking was my mother, but it is my father, that mysterious beauty of him in my every cell, in the animals we both are.

— Dunya, journal entry

Rolling Meditations

The attributes and benefits of Rocking are much the same for Rolling. Rocking is small. Rolling is slow and large.

Suspended Side-to-Side Rolling Meditation

Meditation: Place a thick blanket on the floor. Select smooth music without lyrics, not too quiet and not too active, the quality of a meandering river. Preferably, the music should be a seamless hour-long track without silences to give you plenty of time. Begin reclining on your back, knees bent, feet on the floor. Bring your awareness to your breathing and feel where your back rests on the ground. When you are ready, roll slowly toward one side, letting your legs extend down below you, and over until you are perched on one hip and shoulder, the legs off the ground, and perhaps the bottom arm out in front on the floor to help balance. You will be in elongation. It is as if you are standing full length but placed lying down on the floor. Space surrounds and holds head and legs and the top arm. The body weight presses the flesh of upper arm and side of the hip into the blanket. If you want, roll a bit farther, as if tipping whatever is in your torso out onto the floor. Then gently begin back to supine, the legs folding again and remaining off the floor rather than landing down—so they won't be too heavy as you pass through center. Continue on, legs extending on the side and bending through the middle.

After a while, let the movement subside and rest.

Released Side-to-Side Rolling Meditation

Meditation: Place a thick blanket on the floor. Select smooth music without lyrics, not too quiet and not too active, the quality of a meandering river. Preferably, the music should be a seamless hour-long track without silences to give you plenty of time. Begin reclining on your back, knees bent, feet on the floor. Bring your awareness to your breathing and to where your back rests on the floor. Take some time to soften, letting you body sink into the ground... When you are ready, languidly draw your knees up toward your chest, feet loose in the air, a bit sloppy, hip sockets easy, arms like sleeping pythons on the floor. You can rock gently here, sensing your sacrum on the floor, your shoulder blades. Bit by bit relax toward one side, the knees tipping and descending to the floor, rolling toward one arm, the other arm trailing until it slides gently over as well. Feel everything settle into the ground. Your shoulder, ribs, side of your hip, your forehead. As you begin to roll back to center, be aware of your skull's roundness against the ground. Breathe as you go. Pass through center and roll slowly toward the other side. Feel every little contact with the ground.

Continue rolling slowly, gently from side to side, breathing, breathing, sinking into the floor, melting, your flesh thick as jelly in a sack. Even the bones soften. The ground reaches up to gather you down onto it. Take your time. After a while, let your body move any way it likes, exploring however it wishes. After a while, let the movement subside. Rest.

A Good Night's Sleep

Yesterday evening's practice brought me into Suspended Side-to-Side Roll Meditation. I hung there for an hour, rolling back and forth slowly. I let my mind wander, not focusing too hard. For a while, little daily problems came thick and fast. Then, as I continued, they came in dribs and pops with space in between. That space grew over time. It was like taking a meandering forest walk, not in the vertical but in the horizontal. The effort was distributed along my entire frame. Space, like invisible hands, carried my head. That was lovely. For my body at this time, melting into gravity can exacerbate a few of my tender spots—lower back, one fussy knee that is healing but not yet done. Suspending in this way, I gently handled myself away from pain, passing though many positional variations with support.

Moving slowly and gently always helps minimize jumpy pain response. After moving, I rested on my back for quite a long time. At night I slept deeply, dreamt thick solid dreams, and woke rested, my body fluid and happy.

— Dunya, journal entry

14 MOVEMENT MANTRA: WHIRLING

I can move—and we can all move—beyond my "I", my "my".
Present on our whirling Earth, when are we ever not turning?
— Dunya

The Whirling

Of the Whirling, the Sufis say, "We turn and turn, polishing the heart."
This meditation is a single action. You turn, for a long while. There is a
special way to do it: a placement of hands, a way in the feet, the gaze. I
won't write them down here because the Whirling has been directly
handed from person to person for eight centuries, and though you can
certainly Google videos and copy them, the transmission only comes
from being in the presence of a teacher in the moment. You must find a
teacher who can hand it to you. This is important. However, I can talk
about the Whirling.

Whirling is the motion of our material existence—matter spinning,
gravity pulling in curves. This is our atoms. This is our solar system and
galaxy. People often refer to the dervish Whirling as a movement
metaphor and 'metaphor' may work for onlookers who don't actually
whirl. However, those of us who do the practice of Whirling *experience* the
Universe, cellularly knowing how the cosmos experiences its own
existence. We know its nature, not as a picture, an idea, equations, or
extrapolations. Our flesh vibrates with elemental apperception which is

so potent that practitioners, both novice and seasoned, are impacted by this intimacy and resonance.

Initially, Whirling demands attention. If our focus wanders, we soon teeter and perhaps topple. One power of Whirling is this necessity of attention. There is, in fact, no mental space to invoke a metaphoric image. We do not think about being an atom or a galaxy. We step, step, step, as force grows. We enter the Whirl, and the Whirl gathers us. Caught in the Whirl, momentum holds us upright. A centerline trajectory between Earth's core and the far reaches of the Universe arrows through us while arcs and spirals hold us steady the way the moon orbits Earth. We don't balance and strain and fuss. We don't know how long we've been turning. Time dissolves. We are in the Forever Eternal.

Impact

A dervish turns in white garb. A beautiful performance, beautiful costume. The tall hat, special leather shoes, a long circular skirt hemmed with rope to pull the fabric into a disc is crafted to be seen. But for most turning hours, dervishes whirl in soft, old clothing, in the shadows, feet bare and hair ragged. It is not the look of it, but the true heart heating.

I worked with a large group of practitioners doing a daily Whirling for five days. The last day we all spoke together about how we felt, what we had experienced. No one could wrap it all up. No one had a grip. The impact was too strong to understand. Together we saw this: *I wind and unwind inside. I know something, but I don't know what. A Mystery, a Beauty.* That's as close as I can point, and there is certainly no pinpointing.

In the Marketplace

A fellow Sufi told me about performing the Whirling in a theatre production. She whirled an hour every night while the actors did their acting in the foreground. The play ran for a month. Filmmakers and stage directors often like this idea of whirlers as backdrops—an ancient, cosmic, human symbol. They have no idea the demand on the whirler. When the play closed, my friend slept for a month.

In my solo performances, I often included three or four minutes of whirling. To see a hypnotically turning figure in a long skirt between complex segments of rhythm and design was peaceful for the audience— and for me. I had another reason as well. Even short, performative whirls affected me deeply. My ability to whirl for three minutes didn't come from hours of rehearsal but from hours of whirling as a meditation with my Sufi group, with my teacher. Whirling in performance helped me corporeally remember tenanting mysterious realms in and beyond self. I wanted to revisit these in the midst of the marketplace, sharing its beauty with audiences. Messenger. I wanted to share other mystical movement practices as well—slow movement, for example—but these were unsuccessful in performative context. They are too quiet or take too long, and audiences become restive, impatient.

Pearl in the Heart

Turning and turning with a group, I see time before incarnation and feel comfortable that I will dissolve into the material of the Universe when my incarnation ends. It is lovely, glimpsing at the enormity. Lovely. Shots of rapture linger and linger longer and longer and longer. I whirl. A pearl pierces my heart. Then I stop, sit, melt to the floor. The music seeps into the night wind. The pearl spins in me, its lacre dissolving. The remedy of love spreads heat and stillness and bird trill in every shadow within and without. I love. I love. I love. And love is not so easy for humans, worming its way between fears and foibles, the big chip on every bargaining table. The floor under me has stopped spinning. Now, it turns slowly as it has turned since the Universe's birth.

We turn to the edge of extinction, pause between compassion for our flawed incarnation and dissolution of the deluded ego. That is Sufi work. In the beginning, we dip our toe in dissolution. Rapture floods our giddy hearts. Then, like a dream, it is gone. We grasp at remembered fragments but even those vapor away. This is why many of us seek. We are given the gift. Then we step on the Path and work. We do all that we can do. Why am I here? Why? What am I? We examine ourselves through the lens of actions and interactions, peer at eternity through the window of practice. What is this life? We open and close over and over. The heart must stretch to carry rapture. Eventually rapture subsides into ever-present burbling love, and finally into the widest, most comforting, infinitely inspiring contentment.

— Dunya, journal entry

SECTION TWO: TIME & FORCES

DANCEMEDITATIONS FOR KNOWING

Photo by Paul B. Goode of Teresa Smith

15 SLOW MOVEMENT

Slowness fills us with its syrup.
— Dunya

Slow Movement

Slow Movement is simple, gentle. A slowing down, an easing off. We take more time in the passage of the motion. This simple action—taking more time—can profoundly alter how we experience our experience. Slowing our movement is a savoring of existence. Attending to the entire motion is a savoring. More and more fully we come to dwell in the flavor of our world, inside and out.

Slow Movement Meditation
Meditation: Choose slow, contemplative music. Stand or sit comfortably. Close your eyes and find your breathing. When it is right, begin moving slowly. Bring awareness to the whole movement. Draw attention away from intensity and towards what you are doing. Feel what you are doing, yet feel it lightly. As you continue, let the motion's slowness unfold. Let its slowness grow.

Slow Movement and Savor

It helps to move in an ordinary realm of motion; nothing fancy. Move in a middle range of motion from your centerline—mid-kinesphere movement that is not too vigorous, nor too big, nor too little. Move with enough sensation to know you are there, but not so much that it impedes deepening. At first as we move slowly, we may discover gaps in our stream of sensory feedback. We may skip from motion to motion, or experience a single movement as a dotted line, jumping over the in-between. *Our muscles are like secret drawers crying, "Open me. Open me."* So often we enclose our secrets in numbness, or hide bits of self in jumped-over pockets. Old emotions, surges, trembling, vertigo, immense fatigue may tumble out. Though it is not our goal, Slow Movement may release emotions from unconscious storage. Let them sort themselves out. We aren't in the work of fixing here. We don't sort anything out. We trust our body. Our body knows how to unwind knots of tension the way a cut on your finger heals. You clean it and bandage it, but the body itself knits the skin back together. We need only to pay attention in a relaxed, wondering way.

Slow Movement and Pain

None of us can count on sensibly heeding a pain signal. We typically heed it when we can't ignore it, and we heed it with trepidation. Slow Movement offers the opportunity to learn the difference between pain and intensity, to find the fine edge between pain and intensity, and to move in a sensate subtlety with neither pain nor intensity. We are a self with many layers. A life led with high drama, and intensity blocks perception of subtler layers. How can we feel a delicate sensation if we are doing movement that is painful or intense?

I offer the following question, not to induce self-criticism or guilt, but just an inquiry from self to Self: "Do I use pain and intensity to mask insight and deepening?" I like to ask that because I think deepening is less a high, elitist striving but rather a natural human directive. I think we all go deep. Perhaps we have been given walls and miseries to keep us from the jewels of self-trust and self-knowledge. In any case, pain is an inevitable part of living in a moving body on Earth, but maybe, just maybe, it can be a smaller part. Moving slowly, we undo our overdoing by doing less.

Slower, smaller, less.

Deep State Motion

Oh, to be held and carried in the Subtle Beauty! Slow Movement invites Deep State Motion—a subtle realm of experience. We cannot grab a deep state, however as we slow our movement, relaxing and receiving, we make it possible to be subsumed in Deep State Motion. We can head toward Deep State Motion, yet it comes as a gift. I always feel that it is a communion.

When I studied with Sufi Master, Adnan Sarhan, he conveyed spiritual transmission through Slow Movement. He sat or stood with closed eyes, and we followed his simple slow movements. He would indicate an occasional change with the phrase, "This time." We opened our eyes slightly to see the change then went back to closed eyes. In the moment of seeing the movement, we didn't simply shift from one motion to another, we also received some small seed. Then as we continued the movement with closed eyes, the seed unfolded—tiny secret packets infused with Sufi knowledge delivered kinesthetically. Deep State Motion. I wrote in my memoir *Skin of Glass*, *"Inside Adnan's idiosyncratic movements, in the marrow of the motion, was the Sufi lineage, the energetic stamp called 'transmission'. Shared movement was how he handed that transmission to us. This was dance embedded with the Mystery, dance as a passage to the beyond...."*

16 SPACE, GRAVITY

Dance is a wind blowing through the cells, a river carving the body into curves and cadence.
We swim unaware in an ocean of space until one day, dancing, we wake up drenched.
— Dunya

Space and Gravity

Space and gravity are ubiquitous but invisible. We live in them and they live in us. We lean into air crammed with oxygen and carbon dioxide and nitrogen and helium and dust and ashes. There is no emptiness on Earth. Air clings, capitulates, and captures a gazillion infinitesimal motes that bang into our skin, pushing us slightly left or right, down or up. We blink three times instead of once, and microbes from our pet's exhale wash across our wet eyeball. We imagine that we move about by will, but an approaching thunderstorm has packed the room with moisture and pressure, and this nudges us. Far Space is not far. Not really. Our environment continually impinges. In every motion, we displace space, redirect sound, absorb the slam of light.

The universe weaves and webs lines of force, and our body is a slowing of these dancing lines. Our body, a heavy mat of nerves, bone, tissues, and fluid, is a condensation of ethereal momentum flowing to and from the galaxies. Our body is our network of knowing; feelers crawling everywhere eyes cannot see. The feelers have begun somewhere beyond us; they tangle and twine within us and move out beyond once more. We are not a thing with an inner and an outer; we are a process, a morsel of density maneuvered by distant, massive forces. Our interstitium is a navigational instrument, a navigational dynamic in the universe's navigable field. This field is space. Space not only influences us, it determines us. It creates and sustains us. When we move into our depth, we naturally experience the omnipresent subtlety of Space.

Horizon: Far Space, Near Space, Deep Space, Deep Inner Space

Conceive of space as that which occupies distances. For our exploration of the horizontal, let's consider these regions: Far Space, Near Space, Deep Space, Deep Inner Space. Extend an arm out from your spine and gaze beyond your pointing finger to the topography beyond touch—the corner of the room, a tree in the garden, that ship crossing the bay, a mountain range. At night, our naked gaze regards the Milky Way. All these are Far Space. Our body measures the dimension of Far Space by effort. The farther the distance from our central axis, the more we must stretch, gallop, leap, or dispatch a robotic emissary. In the physical arena, Far Space can only be essayed in small, intense, exhausting, exhilarating doses.

Our ordinary life is lived in Near Space, the close, comfortable region between our centerline and the reach of our limbs. Our hands gesture as we talk, stirring the space. We swim into our sweater, climb into our boots, tumble in our sleep. Near Space is the world of daily doing.

When we close our eyes, we enter Inner Space. Virginia Woolf beautifully says of taking a walk in night's darkness, "...the earth with its infinity of detail [is] dissolved in ambiguous space." What is dark is better felt. We close our eyes and take a deep breath; it is easier to breathe deeply with eyes closed. We close our eyes to hone a thought, to hear a murmur, to sniff a rich scent, to savor a taste. We close our eyes to luxuriate in smooth satin or warm summer beach sand. In this dark, is another seeing, an inward gaze. The tight-knit schemata of visuality frays and dwindles as Inner Space billows. Inner Space is another world of dreams and visions. Most of us have forgotten how to dream in our body. Here, in the flesh, we meet conundrums and inconceivabilities and marvels.

Then we move into Deep Inner Space. As we turn up the dial on subtleties and dim ordinary frequencies, our senses are at once enhanced and diminished. Tiny sounds are loud. We feel the press of air. Scents unwind into their components. The world vibrates and yet we are calm. The environment is not over-stimulating because this Deep Inner Space is far from the surface of existence. In this highly attuned awareness, we meet Far Space once again, this time not as a region of effort but as a continuum. These words border on the description of non-ordinary states because states feel spatial—not in the sense of emotional spaciousness, though that may also be true—but as an *experience* of distances between, regions within, ambient environment, and oneric perception. Space is a place where states exist. After all, we are composed of atoms, and atoms are mostly space. Thus we are mostly space, and space is neither invisible nor empty. It is full and alive.

Near Space, Far Space Meditations
In these meditations we touch the surrounding space, and awaken to how it moves and touches us.

Touching Space Meditation
Meditation: Standing with eyes closed, draw your attention to the space touching your skin. Perhaps at first your face, your hands, your neck, your ankles. Then feel the space between skin and clothing, and outside of the clothing. Begin to move gently, arms lifting away from your body, space coming up under your arms, lifting your arms; space moving between your legs and around your legs as they bend. After a while, see if you can feel the space between your skin and the walls of the room. Take your time. As you invite this perception it will quickly grow.
After a while, relax your attention and let you body move as it wishes.
After another while, lie down and rest.

Carving Space Meditation
Meditation: Sit comfortably, close your eyes, and find your breathing. Draw your focus to your hands. Are they heavy? Light? Where are they resting. Do they want to move or are they tired? Feel how they feel and breathe. When

you are ready, let your hands begin to move in the space in front of you, opening your eyes a sliver to observe your hands between your eyelashes. This time, make each hand into a soft spade shape by closing the spaces between your fingers, the sides of your fingers coming into gentle contact with one another, and the inside of your thumb connecting to the inside edge of your hand. Move these spade-shaped hands through the air in front of you, As you continue, let the air thicken and become gelatinous. Your fingertips carve easily into this viscosity. Don't let the gooey jello slip between your fingers as you explore. In a while, let the space grow dense as if made of clay. How does this change the movement of your hands? The sensation of your hands? Continue carving clay, letting your awareness expand up your arms into your torso.

In a while, relax your attention, relax your hands and let them move however they feel.

In another while, let the movement subside. Lie down, close your eyes, and be at ease, aware of the sensation in your hands and body.

Hands in Space Meditation

Meditation: Sit comfortably. Close your eyes and find your breathing. When you are ready, let your hands begin to move into the space in front of your torso, usually the most natural area for our hands to inhabit. Take your time. Let the hands find their way. What is going on there? In a while, move on to the realm above your head. Close to the skull is different than farther up. Now the space beside your ears. Before your leave this journey, explore the space behind your back. It may be difficult to reach. That is part of our hands' reality. Is there an area which surprises you, a place your hands rarely go? Are some places comfortable? Are some uneasy?

Topography

The spaces—in front, in back, to the side, above—are like different countries with different weather. Let your hands journey and perhaps sojourn here and there. The space beside the ears might remind us that our ears were once gils. The space beside our ribs might remind us that when we were fish, our ribs had fins. Hands relay information about our ambient world to our conscious awareness. As well, our hands continually live and relate to this environment in their own way without our awareness. Independent of volitional instructiveness, hands move from our unconscious the way animals live unseen in the woods.

The Studio

As a young choreographer trained in visuality, I sat at the edge of an empty studio—that is, a studio without furniture, objects, or people. The room was neutral, a potential. A dancer would walk to the center of the room and assume a statuesque shape. I saw the shape she made as well as the space around her. Space was an adornment made apparent by her action. She moved first here then there. The space pinged and exploded and yawned. Even if she stood still, the space woke and uncloaked itself. This was the power of choreography—not only the 'what' of the movements, but the 'where.' I developed elaborate skills within Far and Near Space, finding exquisite ways to visually show space to audiences the way a magician pulls a rabbit from a hat. A viewer could ponder and dream. From growing up with a marine biologist father, I knew that appearances are deceiving, or, more correctly, that our naked eye sees only a small range of existence. He researched microscopic single-celled sea creatures called plankton. Plankton are invisible with ordinary eyesight, but under microscopic magnification, a drop of apparently clear sea water teams with creaturely activity.

I didn't transpose this understanding to human scale space for many years because my job as professional choreographer concerned the representation of ideas, real and abstract. It wasn't necessary to see the vacant studio as it really was—a region packed with microbes and dust and magnetism and particulate. A choreographer's expertise with space exceeds normal day-to-day unconscious habitation of space, but it falls short of the actuality of space. I recently heard a character in a movie exclaim, "Geography is destiny." He meant that one's life is determined by where you were born and raised, but the thought reaches beyond culture. The 'where' of our life—the space—holds us, molds us, moves us. Meditation changed my relationship with dance and my body, awakening my awareness that we not only inhabit space but we participate with it and are largely shaped by it.

Shapes in Space Meditation

Often we approach our interiority as a spacious realm. In this meditation the opposite serves us better; we regard our body as a dense mass in a much less dense space. A sculpture perhaps, though that may be too still. We are breathing and pliable in each quiet form.

Shapes in Space Meditation

Meditation: Use a smooth uneventful music continuum for this. Stand or sit, close your eyes, and find your breathing. Take moment to perceive the whole shape of your body. Feel that shape as you breathe. Now move to another shape—any shape. Be in this new shape for a few breath cycles, feeling your entire body as it inhabits this new shape. Continue on, taking a different shape and remaining for several breath cycles to feel the whole shape. The shape can be extreme or mundane or anything in between. As you continue, you may want to move a little before your settle in the next stillness.

After a while, see if you can feel the space surrounding the mass of your body —between your legs, under your arms—as well as the space surrounding your body. Take your time.

As you continue you may feel a light craving to move. One way to include this while still pursuing the progression of shapes is to inhabit the new shape, then let it ripple slightly the way your reflection might ripple in a slightly disturbed puddle.

After a while, relax your attention and let you body move as it wishes.

After another while, lie down and rest.

This is a quieting variation of the Stop Go game many of us played as children—the one where you run around until someone yells, "Stop!" and you freeze until someone yells, "Go!" That game was all about reflexes and how quickly could you shift from full motion to no motion. In Shape Meditation we have time to transition and time to feel. When we are ready we move from our stillness.

The awareness garnered from this meditation quickly translates to other movement practices and to daily life. As one Dancemeditator said, "The Shape Meditation has informed my 30 year old yoga practice. Changed it really. When I put my body into position now, I think of it as a shape (not as a lunge, for example) and try to fill up that shape from within. It is a whole new way of thinking about the mechanics of it. Or better yet, a way to stop thinking about it altogether." The time with music in your quiet room will awaken embodiment in every space in your day. We are always in a shape. As you read, you are in a shape. You could feel it now from eyes to nose to neck, arms, belly, buttocks, legs, feet.

The morning after offering this meditation to a group and doing it along with them which always deepens my efforts, I sat writing a few reflections in my journal. I expected to notice my hands because I was writing with a pen on paper. This time, however, my lower body felt full and rich though it was quietly folded beneath me. As well, I was aware of the space between me and the wall across the room. I felt situated. According to Sandra Blakeslee, NYTimes science writer specializing in neuroscience and author of *The Body has a Mind of its Own*, our brain continually measures and situates us, elastically mapping us into our rooms and spaces. I think of how my beloved Ric and I experience furniture differently. Ric comes into my studio to chat over his morning coffee. He shifts the bulky armchair to face into the morning sun, then departs leaving the chair slightly off angle. I feel spooked. For me, the chair was as unmoving as a tree or boulder and I navigate through my studio space expecting stable parameters. Now the chair has become a large slow animal. Perhaps Ric lives in a world of such behemoths as this never seems to bother him. Here are a few remarks following a session working with Shapes Meditation:

Karleen: *shape dance...I had a sense of my body in space...not something I am always aware of...*
Gloria: *I found the shape dancing to really allow a deepening into my movement, like it automatically slowed me down. It made me think of ancient cave paintings for some reason, like living fossils of the human story.*
Sandra: *Shapes take me to where I need to be and move thru the wrinkles.*
Jennifer: *Shapes helped me ground and deepen.*

Inner Space, Deep Inner Space
The following two meditations are ways to describe a movement process containing transmission from my Sufi teacher. Even without a teacher, they draw us within where *himma*—spiritual asking—may meet our being gifted. They differ slightly. Both exist in Inner Space and, depending on our depth of concentration, possibly in Deep Inner Space.

Sufi Hands Meditation
In this Sufi meditation, we engage with spatial subtlety though our attention is not specifically on space.

Sufi Hands Meditation
Meditation: With contemplative music playing, sit comfortably and close your eyes, and let your breathing rise to your attention. When you have found your breathing, widen your focus to include your hands. When they are ready, let your hands wake and move slowly in space. Let them find their own way. Let them be relaxed. Let them be soft. Let them be as you watch them with your inner eye. In a while, draw your inner gaze to the inside center of your forehead. (The Third Eye, the pituitary gland.) This time, let your hands move on their own as you watch the blank screen on the inside of your forehead. Always feel the slow, wide ground of breathing. Continue on.
In a while, relax your attention and let your body move however it feels.
In another while, let the movement subside. Lie down, close your eyes, and be at ease, aware of your breathing.

Heart Space Hand Dance Meditation
In this Sufi meditation, we focus on an inner space and the natural radiance residing therein.

Heart Space Hand Dance Meditation
Meditation: With contemplative music playing, sit comfortably and close your eyes, and let your breathing rise to your attention. Move gently from your breathing for a short while, tethering your attention to the breath and the movement. In a while, draw your focus to your heart center. Be aware of its radiant quality as you move. Let the energy from the heart center emanate out through the chest, shoulders, along the inside of the upper arm, along the inside of the lower arm. This current may be warm or hot. It may feel like a liquid or an electrified liquid. In a while, include the palm of the hand in your awareness. As you move, the palms grow warmer and fuller. Continue to bring your attention to this stream of energy surging through the heart center and along the inner arms and palms.
In a while, burrow your attention inward, inside the energetic stream, now

letting this stream carry your hands in space, the elbows lifting and torso floating as if, like a hawk, you are aloft. Let the energy shape the motion while your awareness both submerges more deeply and becomes more acute.
In a while, relax your attention and let your body move however it feels.
In another while, let the movement subside. Lie down, close your eyes, and be at ease. Be aware of your breathing.

Sufi Hands and *Wudad*

I am a nodule on the string of motion that began light years away. I could pretend to not understand this, saying it is mythology because my mind has to struggle and stretch, but my body unwinds and sighs. My body falls into the truth. Space is a truth that cannot be twisted, and meditative movement is a kind of microscope—a microfelt field—to perceive this great subtlety. I remember waking from deep movement meditations at large Sufi gatherings to air that was thick, syrupy, golden. The Arabic word for this—*wudad*—means 'the love in the space'; also, the experience of space activated by a group's meditative efforts, space that is neither cold nor empty nor buzzing nor anxious. The space had been warmed by our collective inner reaching. We had danced with closed eyes, churning and turning, our limbs passing within a hairbreadth yet never crashing or smacking. We sensed one another. Our antennae navigated the blind roil; we were like a murmuration of starlings, that miracle of hundreds of birds swooping and diving as one fluid stream in the gloaming. The birds are not in a unison, which would mean each bird doing the exact same pattern in parallel military precision. No. Each bird does a slightly different path and movement which perfectly harmonizes with the adjacent bird and with the totality of the flock. This collective, comprised of many tiny separate elements, moves as one being. (Some scientists have characterized consciousness as this—many tiny components moving in communion.) We woke after Deep Dancing, not so much a tribe of individuals filled with individual doses of endorphin, but as a collective that has navigated as a one entity. We watched the *wudad* in stillness. We saw space transformed. A truth. A magic revealed.

Our deepest dancing brings Far Space into Deep Inner Space and vice versa—a 'changing' and a 'being changed' of the distant and inner fields. We don't dissolve into Far Space because we never left it. We are not separate because it creates us. Every fragment of existence is the folding and pressing and yawning and pulling of space. Spiritual traditions fond of the phrase "I surrender" fumble with an unnecessary piety. Of course we surrender; we have no choice; we are formed by magnetism and momentum.

Vertical: Low Space, Middle Space, High Space

We skitter along Earth's crust caught in its spin, its gravity, its magnetism. If it stopped, we'd be stripped away into space. We turn and bend and walk at the beck and call of these intractable forces.
— Dunya

Low Space, Middle Space, and High Space are, in essence, three relationships to gravity. (Using the word 'space' gives a spherical feeling to our felt understanding.) I define these areas very loosely and simply as the distance your head is from the center of the Earth (excluding inverted positions where your head would be lower than your heart or pelvis.) Low Space is the area along the floor. Middle Space is the area midway between standing and lying down which encompasses sitting, kneeling, and crawling in a quadrupedal or four-footed stance. High Space is standing in the bipedal or two-footed stance and includes locomoting (moving through space) and jumping. Traversing these three spaces is to travel the map of our planet's creaturely evolution.

Our interstitium, which is the fascia interweaving our entire body, continually responds to Earth's gravity, and Earth's whirling around our Sun by way of gravity and centripetal force. Our Sun, in turn, is in a magnetic cosmic relationship to adjacent cosmic systems, and they are in a relationship to their other neighbors, and so forth. We are thereby subtly touched by distant bodies. Independence is merely a notion. Our meditative practice may help us engage little used parts of our brain, maybe an ancient birdbrain. Birds migrate by means of infrared patterns. Bats zoom about using sonar. Sightless people––the blind––use a cane to walk in the world but can often navigate familiar spaces by sonar and temperature and air pressure or perhaps other capacities we have not thought or known to measure. There are many ways of seeing.There are many capacities for navigating and situating the self. With practice, these deep brains can awaken. We move, we engage, and as we move, we are moved. Our interstitium is an interdependence.

We rarely know that Andromeda is touching us, tapping us; yet moving with greater spatial awareness wakes us. After, we stumble less, walk irregular landscapes with a sure step. At night, we might move in the dark, oriented and stable, our feelers sensing the wider web of which we are a component. It feels like ocean swimming. We all know this sensation of being pushed and floated by swells and waves, our body a small flotsam in the large sea. That is life in air and space as well, all mediated by our connection to gravitational force.

My work with Mary Bond, Structural Integration specialist and author of two wonderful books, *Your Body Mandala* and *The New Rules of Posture*, has helped me follow intuitive impulses emerging from my tissues to delve fully into the exploration of gravity. Since in our mundane life, we tend to stand or move through High Space, sit for many hours in Middle Space to do computer work or drive, and lie down to rest or sleep in Low Space, we will open tremendous possibilities for ourselves by spending exploratory movement time in each of these spaces. Each space gives our body an opportunity to experience new or forgotten pathways neglected by our daily routines. In your creative unfolding with gravity, you may discover the need to stay with one level for a longer time. That is a wonderful calling. Immerse fully. And then, come back to offering the body time in all three.

Simple Gravity Meditation

Meditation: Our purpose is to experience gravity—the weight, the lightness—and to let our bodies accommodate and savor the range of demand between weight and lightness. Use any music you wish that will support your motion without requiring your attention. For the next half hour, occupy each of the three areas—Low Space, Middle Space, High Space—spending ten minutes in each, doing any movement your wish, feeling the sensation of gravity. After, relax your attention and move freely.
In a while, rest.

Lush Gravity Meditation: Low then High and Middle Spaces

Here is a fuller exploration of vertical spaces. I write these as two different meditations, but I recommend doing them sequentially as part of one practice session; the contrast between Low and High helps us more easily perceive gravity and activate interstitial support. Spend an extended period in Low Space, follow with High Space, then complete your practice with Middle Space. I articulate apparently unusual foci for

High Space inspired by Mary Bond's suggestion of accessing the lightness of our spine's upward reach through our ears, and combine this with foot soles resting into the ground.

Low Space Meditation
Meditation: Find gentle steady music. Prepare a large padded floor surface; it shouldn't be so cushioned that the sensation of the floor is too muted or muffled but no so thin that the floor surface causes discomfort. Lie down can supine (on your back) or prone (on your belly) or your side. Close your eyes. Find your breathing. When you are ready begin to move slowly, feeling that gravity holds you, carries you as you gradually move. Do any sort of movement. You might undulate along your spine, or softly, slowly squirm, or roll. As you move, bring your awareness to how you connect to the ground. Perhaps the ground is like an enormous serpent swelling beneath you, shifting you as it shifts.
Give yourself plenty of time with this. As you progress, let go into gravity. Let the ground hold you, massage you. If you need, pause and be at ease from time to time.

High and Middle Space Meditation
Meditation: After an extended period in Low Space, bring yourself to standing. Stand on both feet with your eyes closed or barely open. Take a little time to feel the difference between being close to the ground and now being upright on the small pedestal of two feet. Feel the feet melted into the floor. Sway gently, feeling your weight shift, aware of the contrasting weight and lightness in your body.
In a while, while still feeling your feet, bring your attention to your ears. They are two curved flower-like structures nestled on either side of your cranium. Let the invisible line between them float your head in space. Continue gently swaying.
This time, simultaneously feel the curved shape of your foot soles on the ground and the curved shape of your ears. They are similar. Continue swaying, feeling both your ears in High Space and foot soles resting into gravity in Low Space. The ears connect to the horizontal and the foot soles to the vertical.

Feel how these two areas suspend you in space and root you to the ground. Continue this for a while. This is our body in High Space.

If you wish, you can extend your attention to include an inwarding into the depths of the ears and an upwarding into the columnar ankle.

In a while, sit on a chair, your feet resting on the ground. Be aware of the feet of your pelvis—your still bones—as well. Most of our weight now rests of the feet of the pelvis. Take some time moving gently in Middle Space, feeling gravity resting into our seat. Continue for a little while, then relax your attention.

Move any way you wish or lie down and rest.

Thoughts About Low Space

Large swathes of body surface touch the ground. Gravity acts directly on arm or spine or foot. We are a snake, a worm, a slug. Our fluids flow easily back and forth like rivers. Distant vision is limited, but our surface awakens as skin brushes and drags. The skin sensation connects directly to our fascia. Though the sensation of fascia is subtle, with attention it will come forward into our perception. *Do we succumb to the surface? Do we hold ourself off the surface? How does the surface feel? Supportive? Irritating? Too hard, too soft, too unrelenting, too anything? Or does it feel like it rescues you? Does it have a life of its own in relation to you?* Moving in low space along the floor brings many feelings.

In her book *Sensing, Feeling and Action,* Bonnie Bainbridge Cohen says, "Whatever people can't do on their belly, they're going to have trouble with in a higher pattern, meaning higher level from the floor. You can come across a movement problem on the vertical plane, someone standing, and trace it to a developmental pattern that can be worked through lying on the belly (horizontal plane)."

Thoughts About High and Middle Space

As we move in High Space, our fluids pump up and down. We orient ourselves through hearing. If our eyes were open we would see far distances. A lot depends on our feet. So much weight and balance is handled by the slender ankles and delicate foot bones. I remember the surprise reverberating in me when Mary Bond remarked, "The entire leg is a foot!"

In Middle Space, we may sit or kneel. This stable plane offers many options for balance and effort. Or perhaps we are on our hands and knees or seated on one hip and leaning on one hand, experiencing complex counterbalances.

Falling and Rising Meditation

Because transitioning between low and high space is physically challenging, this meditation requires steady, undeviating focus, though not a heavy-handed focus. The effort helps clear a wandering mind.

Falling and Rising Meditation

Meditation: Choose legato, sustained music. Begin standing. Find your breathing. Let the eyes be open with an unfocused gaze. When you are ready, descend slowly and steadily to the floor into a full recline. Find the most efficient path. Move in one continuous, slow flow. Then rise to standing with arms reaching above you. We might ooze down with the quality of cool honey, then rise slowly up like thick fog. Do at least three rounds.

Though we are flesh and blood creatures, we have within us honey and fog. Find these flavors. Find a languid sense of the full motion, unhurried, suspended, slow but not painful or strained. Find the way that honey and fog luxuriate in relation to gravity. That is the actual sense of gravitational force on our body. As well, experiment with the pattern of motion through which you rise and fall. You might spiral up-and-down; you might be able to do a straight jacket knife-ing up and down; you might pass through long lunges. After a while, our options may increase. I suggest at least three rounds in the session because round one is typically a bit ungainly.

As we grow stronger, we can do more rounds. Personally, I find the first couple of days with Falling and Rising Meditation a bit bumpy. It isn't just a matter of strength; I seem also to lack the wholeness of the motion. However, within a short period of repetition, my body finds its totality, acting in concert, unfolding sequentially and seamlessly, all of itself supporting itself. Legato, sustained music helps slow the motion down, but beware music that is too soporific which might encourage dropping out once you reach the floor. We need a bit of energy in our musical support. This is especially true of longer periods with the meditation.

SECTION THREE:
DREAMING IN THE FLESH

DANCEMEDITATIONS FOR EXCAVATION & EXPLORATION

17 THE IMAGINAL REALM

Dancemeditation is to the body as dreaming is to the mind.
— Dunya

I Would Hate to Never Dream

I would hate to never dream, to never wonder as I wake where I've been, to not grasp at dim air, the fading figures amused at my futile attempts to catch their tail. I love the improbability of making sense of their portentous magic which flattens and dulls as I note it in my journal, losing its weave of one place tucked into another, actions looped, and haunting fragments pastiched across timelines. Dreams come while we lie still, our bodies suspended in sleep as our mind roams far and wide. What if dreams came as we moved? Our body wants more than therapies, a hot bath, a massage, a walk, a workout, more than shoes and clothes and a comfy bed where it sleeps while our minds churn along. What does our body also love? The body also loves to dream. The following meditations activate our delicious somatic imagination through imagery, sensation, flashlight focus, and elemental trajectories. When we free our flesh from ordinary, task-based experience, we let it explore, excavate, discover, and dream.

The imaginal realm—we use image to ignite felt exploration. Images reach beyond 'looking like.' They ignite 'behaving the same as,' 'moving in the same way as.' Images ignite cellular affinity and engage our body's totality far more than any fitness machine or mental strategy. Here are three nature images with fruitful possibilities: a slow viscous animal, a root growing and exploding into air, and an underwater marine plant. These choices steer away from visual fascination and toward rich, uncommon sensation. What is more important, they were experientially harvested not from screen or photographic image but from walking in a forest or by the ocean. The greater the image source's dimensionality, the fuller our motion experience.

Slug Meditation
The Slug invites us to sink into gravity and groundedness.

Slug Meditation
Meditation: Relax onto the ground, close your eyes. Feel into your breath. Let gravity sink you way, way down. After a while, when you've let go of some of your resistance to gravity, let the image of slug come in. Take your time. Let the image find its place inside of you and begin its work. Keep going…the creature unfolding in your flesh.

This meditation came to me at a Dancemeditation Weekend in California. In the first half of a day-long session, after moving slowly with narrow focus for 1 ½ hours, participants slept without stirring or fussing in deep, seamless quiet. I kept watch, feeling what to do next, casting about inside myself, not because I was impatient or insecure about letting quiet and rest linger, but because, like the faint rumble of an as-yet-unseen airplane in the fog, I sensed the next activity approaching.

Then I felt a nudge and remembered walking a dappled path in an old growth forest in Oregon, ensconced in verdure, the giant trees coated in moss and footed by ferns. At the edge of a needled path, a fat banana slug paused. I squatted down beside him and reached out my forefinger to gently touch his gleaming flank. He was cool and strong. He swiveled one eyestalk. I snatched my hand back and was surprised at how the sensation of his being continued to sing in my fingertip. Now, several days later in another city, a sense memory of the banana slug still hummed in my forefinger. Here was the action that had been approaching come fully into my mind; perhaps we could explore the wonder of this creature into our bodies in this workshop, feeling his thickness, heaviness, coolness, the ground, the sluggishness. I share this to illustrate image sourcing. I knew Slug was a rich image for a body because my body—not my head—had recalled it. Images are all around. Rather than grabbing with your mind, let them come to you. This is what happened for me once I began exploring this image on my mat...

On the Ground

On the ground, I enter a world of topographies, tugs, touches, textures that my feet never notice as they fleetly ramble along in their shoe casings. My belly, the skin on my inner arms, my flank, the back rim of my shoulders, or the tops of my bare feet delicately touch the wool carpet, tasting the rough even-ness. My viscera's liquidity slowly thickens into slug-like muscularity. I progress through time. I sink down. I inch and ooze, absorbed into the drag along the carpet. My bones soften. Its organized, layered systems melt into a chewier, simpler morsel of animal. Pointy thoughts round and roll, gelatinous in the head bowl. I am a creature unlike myself, in a world of incrementality and surface. At some point, I stood and transposed the horizontal into the vertical, leaning into space and air, attenuating the sensorial memory of the ground as I moved upright. I filled with wonder. I was in wonderment. A delighted glee popped in my cells—my body in something new, in the irreverence of release from the servitude of logic which my mind loves to occupy and impose. My body dreaming.

— Dunya, journal entry

The Vine Meditation

A vine connects the ground and all that lies compressed and unlit beneath us, with our natural sense of reaching up into space, air, and light.

The Vine Meditation

Meditation: Close your eyes and bring your attention to your breathing. Feel yourself breathe in and breathe out. Do three full breath cycles, feeling all of yourself, all of the breath. Now, bring your focus to your feet. Breathe and feel them planted like seeds in soft soil. Root fibers grow down and down into cool quiet darkness. Breathe in and out. Let the earth's energy begin to stir in your feet. Feel the presence of the Vine. Root hairs spread down. Pale tendrils begin their slow upward climb. The vine uncurls into our ankles, winding through our tendons, spreading beneath skin, permeating muscles, twining around bones. As they climb and twine they move us. Ankles, calves, knees, thighs soften into vines. The vine winds through hip sockets, girdles hips, meanders through viscera, along the spine. Is your spine a vine? Our torso twines, and leaves unfurl, the tendrils snaking through arms and hands and up into neck and head and everywhere all at once. The vine blooms. Wide leaves and feathery leaves, lush flowers, bright berries, fragrance, juice, abundance.

Like our fascia—our connective tissue—the Vine is curvilinear. We store our experiential memories in our fascia. Moving in the vine motif aligns with the natural construction of our fascia and helps resolve tension.

The Vine in Art & in the Wild Garden

The archetypal vine motif has embellished art since the misty beginnings of human time. What is the vine? It points its winding finger toward lavish palatial ornamental grounds, and toward a small, intimate garden where a trembling tendril climbs a trellis. A vine might be tame as in Islam where, gracefully and intelligibly twined, it symbolizes infinite Paradise. In fairy tales, the wild vine is Chaos, an incomprehensible tangle of forbidding and fear—that snarled mass around Sleeping Beauty. Because vines often have no discernible beginning or end, they often signify Timelessness. As you enter the idea of the Vine, and the Vine enters your body until your body becomes the Vine, feel the energy of growth, the effortlessness of natural unfolding. What does your vine do? Where does it go? How does it feel? What is your vine today?

I wrote this after one practice: "Today I dance to Arabic taksim. The music hypnotizes me into the Moment. Vines of sound coil this way and that, furbelows and twists and double-backs and digressions. The flute takes me. We wind around and around, losing our bearings. As if in a blizzard, the world swirls white. I seem to waltz on the same spot, step after step, heading somewhere but which way? The world becomes spherical. The relentlessness of linear time has dissolved....When the snowfall ends, when the music resolves, the world stills. I am somewhere, but is it forward or backward or up or down? I am just here."

Sense Memory. I can tell you, Vine Meditation transformed from everything I just mentioned above when one winter I spent two months clearing wild overgrowth in my back garden. I went at it ripping and clipping. At some point after the initial hack job, I saw no way forward short of killing every desirable tree and shrub as collateral damage except to patiently unwind, snip, then extricate shortened lengths of the five to ten foot strands. Bittersweet, Porcelain Vine, Cat Briar, bramble, Virginia Creeper, Evergreen Spindle, ivy, wild rose, honeysuckle, mile-a-minute vine, and clematis entwined in fibrous, impossibly complex mats. In the evenings, I moved with closed eyes on my sheepskin, my body inhabited by a multidirectional melange of movement. The back yard vines that had scratched and tangled me by day coursed through me at night. This was a huge shift in consciousness. I had previously done this practice instructing myself to move in ornamental, comprehensible curves. Now I was embroiled in the inscrutability of vine-age, its reality less rigid and concrete than my initial engagements and far more reflective of its truth which in turn opened my body's "undulating aqueous layers of awareness." (Phillip Lopate, author of *Portrait of My Body*)

So, much as I appreciate the first approach, I prefer the second. Let an image come to you with this much chew and whiff. Connect with your entire body to something real. Let it work in you.

Seaweed Meditation

The spine in space resembles seaweed in an ocean.

Seaweed Meditation

Meditation: The image—seaweed attached to a rock on the seafloor. I usually use sustained spacious Indian classical flute music that meanders gently to provide a sonic oceanic ambience. Sit anywhere—on a chair or the floor in any comfortable position. Dim your gaze, eyes partially closed and unfocused so that the room grows shadowy. Whatever touches the sitting plane is the rock. It can gently roll and shift, moved by deep, cool current. The spine begins low at the sacrum. It is the seaweed. Find an under ocean plant to let into your flesh.

I began using the rockweed of Maine coastal waters with its thick dark olive green spatulas that tether securely to rounded, rounded granite boulders, feeling my spine as a dense central stem out of which my arms and head grew, but there is an enormous submarine garden. Brilliant green, feathery Mermaid's Hair. Dark strands of Eel grass. Meaty ropes and wide rubbery fans of Devil's Apron String—kelp.

A human body and seaweed body are multicellular with architecture.

Bones and muscles and skin and organs in one, central stem and alveoli and leaves in the other. As well, these creatures' environments share commonalities. Both ocean and air are molecular with currents flowing throughout, are shaped by thermal streams and layering, and suspend particulate. With our attention it is possible to not only transpose our body into the seaweed and emulate, but more crucially to discover our self in its more primordial form, a way we once were, a way in which those traces still whisper in us, a way in our current incarnation of remembering and re-experiencing our creaturely ancestry. We come to know that we still are seaweed in an ocean, just the way delving into our unconscious helps us understand that we are still an infant and a teenager. We contain now all that has come before and can find within our motion, the motions and patterns of our creature lineage.

18 THE NARRATIVE REALM

Our bodies murmur day and night, and sometimes these murmurings matter.
— Dunya

The Narrative Realm

By rights, the Narrative Realm is the purview of theatre and psychodrama. While the following meditations may therapeutically unearth our personal unconscious, their intent is wider. We enter a hidden theatre marching invisibly side-by-side, beneath, and beyond the obvious. Many of the following exercises employ a silk veil—a swath of lightweight silk, 3 ½ yards long, 45" wide—that acts as a 'feeler' expanding us beyond our body's skin edge. Silk is sensitive; it reads spatial whispers and, like a cosmic fishing net, swallows ghosts and messengers from the Unknown, to cast them into our awareness.

Veil Skills

Genius comedian, Robin Williams, did a classic theatre exercise during an interview. He jumped up, grabbed a pink pashmina from an audience member and maniacally turned himself into twenty characters in seven minutes, punctuating a barrage of accents with drape, swing, wrap, and whip of that little strip of fabric. A tour de force! Veil Shapeshifter Meditations reimagine our length of silk in just this way while Skill

Drills help us become acquainted with how our veil moves. Spend a little time for pleasure but also to get to know silk which is, literally, its own animal.

Veil Skills Meditations
Toss & Catch: Toss the veil balled up, then catch it, open it out, find and hold the selvage in your fingertips.
No Fingers: Move with veil without using your fingertips to hold it.
Drop & Gather: Drop the veil then pick it up from floor without using fingertips.
Veil in Air: Move without letting the veil touch floor.
Painting the Wind: The veil is a pen or paintbrush and space the surface to paint or write on. With an open, inclusive, neutral gaze, observe the beauty of the fabric, the play of color in space.

Veil Shapeshifter Explorations

These explorations expand our relationship with this shapeshifter. No longer laundry, the veil is a partner and a world—inviting experience that may not be intelligible or sequential yet may feel narrative. There may be scene-like images, an interplay of 'this, then that' which, like dreams, make no typical time-based sense yet inexplicably belong together. The veil may unravel a miasmic, non-specific mood. As we loosen into the silk, we become Beauty in the Beast's unearthly Castle, stories breathing and twining into the silk, our skin, the air.

Veil Shapeshifter Meditations
Dressing: The veil is a cloak, shawl, or clothing. Explore washing and dressing. Does it bind you, envelope you, burden you, hide you?
Shroud: A meditation on death and protection. Being inside the silk. Contained in the self and disconnected from outer space.
Billow: Veil fills like a sail on the inhale and subsides on the exhale. A huge gill. Sheer Abyss creatures.
Dialogue: Veil is a partner, being, or condition with which you dialogue. Perhaps it is an antagonist with who you must come to resolution. Perhaps a nemesis. Perhaps a beloved.

Creatures: Let the veil be a baby or a bird or a snake. How do you sojourn with this creature?

Things: Let the veil be a flag. Let the veil be a streamer. Let the veil be a whip. Let the veil be a rope. Wide, narrow, heavy, light. Do you drag or haul, hoist or heave? Each thing is so different.

Landscape: Drape the veil along the floor bunched up or elongated. It is now a river or stream or path or pool. You have a landscape to travel and inhabit.

Atmosphere: Can the veil be fog, smoke, mist?

Situation: Let the be veil a refuge, safe and comforting, a relief. Now, let it be danger, confusion, miasma.

Wing: The veil is wing. As you turn and arc and whirl, feel how you expand into space, your reach extending beyond your fingertips. Perhaps you glide over the ground more lightly because the veil breathes loft your core. In a while, drop the veil and continue moving. Feel how this feels.

Watching Kate

At one Movement Monastery retreat, we did Veil Witnessing—two groups, one watching as the other moved, then alternating roles. The group of movers used their veils. I watched someone bind their legs and feet and struggle. Another person laid their veil long on the floor and became a disconsolate wanderer crossing and re-crossing that river. Kate, who is an herbalist, playwright, and all-round imaginative, deep-souled witch, dragged a many-hued silk veil along the ground as if it weighed two hundred pounds. Suddenly she flipped it up into a plume of rage before sinking to the ground where her spine bent in sorrow. She slowly scoured the floor, the silk balled up. I don't know remember the actual color of her veil, but in memory it took on a dark garish red, ruddy and sodden, and I knew she was mopping up blood. In the talking circle that followed, Kate related how the veil had unfolded a narrative on its own. In the veil dance, she had murdered her abusive husband, dragged him into the forest, then gone back to clean up the murder scene.

Veil as Companion

One time, a person said of their veil, "My veil has always seemed like a dear pet. When I dance with her, she often leads, and I am fond of her beyond imagining." Someone else spoke of moving companionably with her veil, "Such spontaneous, natural, effortless exchange, riding the crest of novelty, each moment a new unfolding." The surprise here is the emergence of our veil influencing us. As another person reminded me, "So-called inanimate objects have a life, a consciousness, if only we attune to this."

Maybe you've done one of the above cues, or not. Perhaps instead you have paced patiently but impatiently around your private space, the veil lightly gathered in one hand like a small furred, rabbit-y creature with a long trailing tail. Perhaps your feet slide into the musical beats as if into slippers. And after a while your notice that the hand carrying the rabbit-y creature is warm and quiet while the other hand trails its fingers though pools of cool air. As if waking from a daydream, except you feel more like you've entered a daydream, your two hands live in different worlds and, *ping!*, something happens inside....The feet crisscross, or the airy hand swings up, fingers curling around an invisible rose poised on an invisible stem overhead, plucks it, and coils it down from the sky as the bunched veil glides forward to catch this blossom, an offering to what you don't know, but you know it is an offering. You are in a forgotten garden. *How did I get here?* The veil spills from your hand like rose water.

If we go along, waiting, patiently or impatiently, such wonderment will likely come. No promises, of course. Why is this good? Maybe for you it isn't, but for me it is a place in the heart of Hearts. Because it is a miracle to be in the Moment, in the Precious Beauty. Robert Kaplan, journalist and political traveloguer, writes in his powerful book *Balkan Ghosts* of the difference between Western Christianity and Eastern Orthodoxy. "While Western religions emphasize ideas and deeds, Eastern religions emphasize beauty and magic." I read Kaplan's work long after I'd begun my delving into Eastern mysticism where my hunger for, and pleasure in, Beauty & Mystery—a word closer to mysticism than 'magic'— found its home. So, for me, such Beauty, such Mystery, is core sustenance.

As I or you or we dance into our depths, the part where we focus on an idea, a cue, a meditation is the period of Relaxation, letting go of stress bit by bit. That is moving the veil. Receptivity is the pivot of consciousness. We open. We let it happen.

That is what I mean when I write of the companion in the forgotten garden.

The Lover in the Veil

I turn and back away.
A billow curves in my wake.
He is the curve. He hovers, arched in the invisible air.
I love him so utterly
that I must turn
and turn again
and back away with a billow in my wake
to see him lingering like a smile in the space...

If I keep moving we will never be apart.
When I stop, he is gone,
a fire when it is nothing but ashes.

But in turning and curving
he loves me with his movement,
his sliding around and filling out,
his body coming to cling to me, kissing me
everywhere with a thousand silk lips
until, turning and curving,
the air comes between us making room for space
and I see him smiling in my wake.

Sometimes he is a snake
hanging his limb over my neck
and falling onto my arm,
into my hand
which cannot hold him enough
to quench my desire
for his wisdom,
for his fluid obedience,
for his airy obeisance.
He bows to my whim yet he is my master
for he is only mine when I call him with all myself.

I am thirsty for his wrapping!
But then, exhausted with twining,
in the cool coils of his sibilant arms,

I see that I've exhausted him as well.
He is gone, an empty skin left behind
to keep my bones and blood company
and I sink to that oblivion where all things meet
in the warm dark of depth.
— Dunya

Contemplative Veil Meditations

These gentle quiet meditations are a balm for anxious times when we need a sweet sojourn away from worries.

Veil & Hands Meditation

Meditation: Sit crossed legged with the veil draped on your lap and on the floor in front of you. With the veil as backdrop, let your hands move above it. Breathe gently and deeply. As your hands move against the veil backdrop, draw the view in and out through your eyes, inhaling and exhaling, gently watching.

Glacial Veil Meditation

Meditation: I say glacial, because slow is never slow enough. Stand holding the veil in any way that allows you move slowly without dropping or needing to fuss with the fabric. Now, move glacially. As you move, sense the entire shape and presence that you and the veil make together.

Veil Witness Dances with a Partner or in Groups

What seems true for this meditation is the perceptual uniqueness of each person. The veil augments each Mover's uniqueness without them having to push outward in their consciousness. They can stay comfortably within their flow, inside their world. As they move, the Witness sees the Mover larger than life, less hidden, less covered despite the use of a covering-like prop. For the Mover, this feels very different than Slow Movement focusing on an inner state, which might be softer, more suspended, drifting under water.

Veil Witness Dance with Partner Meditation
Meditation: Take a partner. One person is the Mover, and the other The Witness.

Mover, move slowly, glacially. Perhaps, Mover, pause in the slow flow from time to time to feel the shape that your body and the veil are making. Mover, empty the interior sense of your body and become a husk. Focus attention on the sensation of your body's periphery. Body and veil are a moving sculpture. You might appear to be caught in ice. Witness, sit comfortably, find your breathing, and let your gaze relax. While you are witnessing, be at ease and gently be aware of your body.

Change roles. Each round goes 10-15 minutes.

After, sit and share with another your experience as Mover and as Witness.

Glacial Veil Witness in Groups
Meditation: Before picking up the veil, do a strong period of extremely slow movement with the intent of the entire body being empty, as if it is a shell. The body is a moving sculpture, a carapace caught in ice. Be aware of the shape created by veil and body together. This is very different from Slow Movement focused on an inner state; there the body might have a soft, suspended appearance as if drifting underwater.

Now divide into two groups. Witnesses sit around the edge of the space while Movers take the center. Movers move glacially, periodically pausing or stopping. In the paused moment, be aware of the body's shape and the shape the veil is making.

After 15 minutes, change roles.

For each of us individually, our veil is inherently relational, being always an 'other.' That is the Mover's experience. Witnessing is entirely different and it is not our job to see what the Mover or Movers intend. We see what is there for us. Witnessing is its own rich world. Witnessing one person and witnessing a group bring starkly divergent gifts. When we split into two groups, one group moving glacially and each individual mover moving with their own veil, the witnessing group sees a collective humanity evoking human history, societies, cosmologies.

19 ORCHESTRAL BODY

...if bones were secrets, if skin was air
if eyelashes were daggers, and knees were prayers,
if the spine was a ladder dropping down in the well,
if calves unrolled like ancient scrolls...
— Dunya

Our Orchestral Body

An orchestra has stringed instruments and tympani, a brass section of braying trumpets and crooning French horns, and woodwinds. So many different tonalities, voices, all composed into order, the music coming out as sonic paintings or rousing calls to action, playing together, but not mashed potatoes. Our body is an orchestra of different voices. Each part —hands and feet, legs and arms, head, neck, back and belly, to name the obvious arenas—has a different role in the action of our daily life. Each body part has evolved to a purpose. This we all know, but each body part also has a distinct capability beyond its function. Each body part has a voice, often is full of its own imagination, its own dreams, its own lamentation. In our time on the mat, we can explore our somatic realm part by part. Then our body stops being mashed potato and becomes orchestral.

Hands

50% of the brains' motor cortex (it sits like a headband on the top of the head) controls the hands and face.
—*Teresa Hawkes, PhD, Neuroscience*

Hands are our most comfortable, familiar body part. Even the shyest person can do a Hand Dance. Yet, despite this natural eloquence, we confine hands to daily toil. How delicious to let them explore and talk to us. When given free rein, hands readily engage in surprising, personal dances.

Hand Meditations

For the following meditations, imaginative, colorful music with varied moods and rhythms opens the dreams in our hands.

Right Hand, Left Hand Meditation

Meditation: Sit comfortably. Close your eyes and find your breathing. When you are ready bring your attention to the right hand and let the left hand rest. Feel how the right hand feels and, when it is ready, let it move any way it likes. It may ride on the music, float without shape, or aimlessly meander. Hands usually go on their own journey fairly easily, but to move beyond a bossy mind's doing-ness can take time even for the most seasoned practitioner. Patience here. In its own good time, the hand opens up to you. After a while, let the movement subside and the right hand come to rest. Be at ease for a bit. Note the sensation in the right hand, then in both hands, observing without altering.

This time, it is the left hand's turn to move, to feel itself. Set it going on its journey. Is it different? Likely yes, as it leads a different worldly life. Bear witness as this hand unfurls its secret life. After a while, let the movement in the left hand subside, the hand coming to rest. Feel how they feel.

Now, let both hands move but instead of going immediately to mirrored symmetry, allow each hand its individuality while simultaneously moving. They have just expressed themselves one at a time; now let them continue side-by-side in their difference. This takes a bit of attention but isn't as hard as you might imagine. (Like a pianist. Like you when you chop an onion.)

Finally, invite both hands move together any way they like.

Each hand has its own identity and distinct way of moving. At first these unmatched beings occupying apparently matching limbs may be strangers, or at least we feel strange that they've been hiding *sub rosa.* Logic will tell us we shouldn't be surprised. Our hands accomplish differing worldly tasks and have ingrained different patterns, however in this meditation we sense that each hand has a very different connection to our being, beyond handed-ness and beyond right and left hemispheric brain orientation. Once we sink below our cognitive threshold, hands become beings we often do not recognize. Strangers in our flesh. Visitors. I sometimes feel like a medium with spirits gesturing into me, laden with semaphore.

Fingertip Hand Dance Meditation

Meditation: Sit comfortably, close your eyes, and find your breathing. You may have music playing or not. Bring your awareness to your hands. Be aware of their weight, what surface is touching what, their temperature. Feel all this as you breathe. When you are ready, let your hands move away from any surface they are touching and hover in the space in front of you. Open your eyes a sliver and softly gaze through your eyelashes at your hands. This time, gently move your hands from side to side in front of you, the way you would brush smoke from the air. Settle this motion into the rhythm of your breathing. As you continue this parallel hand motion, touch the thumb tip and forefinger tip together. This makes a teardrop shape, or an eye. The other three fingers are softly separated. Continue, feel the feeling of two fingertips meeting.

This time, continue the parallel motion and touch the thumb and middle fingertip together. What feels different? Take your time, the breathing supporting the side-to-side motion. In a while, touch thumb and ring fingertip together, feeling the circle their connection makes. Lastly, the thumb and baby finger together. Here the palms fold like a half open leaf. How do the other fingers feel?

Next, cycle through the finger tip touches, one after the other. As you continue, allow the hands to find other spatial tracks. The hands might mirror one other, or move in opposition. Let them move in whatever way helps you feel what you are doing, and to better experience your experience.

In a while, let your hands do whatever they want to do.

When you are full, lie down, close your eyes, and be at ease. Rest.

Poem of Hand Dances

I found these jotted in my journal, some noted midway through my movement practice to explore, and others which my body had discovered on its own, afterward. Perhaps your hands will enjoy them. As always, sit comfortably, find your breathing, and, with music you like, let your hands begin to play. Do a few, or just one. At the end, let your hands go into their own worlds and dreams.

> *My hands are daggers. My hands are trowels.*
> *My hands are needles and hammers.*
> *My hands are talons, pincers, and claws.*
> *My hands are roses, then paws.*
> *My hands are flames. My hands are tongues.*
> *My hands are ferns and fans.*
> *My hands are pages and mirrors and eyes.*
> *My hands are wings and wands.*
>
> *My hands skitter and scatter and slice.*
> *And stroke, and pierce, and grind.*
> *They carve, they drape, they gather, they float.*
> *They caress. My hands are mine.*
>
> *My hands are limp.*
> *My hands are stiff.*
> *My hands are tense and dense.*
> *My hands are secretive, whispery, vague.*
> *My hands are fragile, liquid, and soft.*
> *My hands are perishable.*
> *My hands are lost.*

Feet Meditations

How many of us actually think of our feet? Unless you are hobbled by bad shoes or plantar fasciatus, or are a ballet dancer honing feet to articulate like hands and shoot you into the air, most feet in this world plod and pace and pound. Most are left collecting blood under the table, thickening on car peddles, or swelling on airplanes. Most feet are forgotten.

Stationary Feet Meditation
Stationary Feet Meditation stimulates liveliness in spine, hips, head, neck, helping us feel the connection between feet and ground. It roots us. Whenever we limit the motion in one area of our body, the other areas will discover new patterns. The feet are an especially potent area on which to impose restrictions because we move them so much in our day-to-day actions, as well as our dancing.

Stationary Feet Meditation
Meditation: Select infectious rhythmic music that isn't hectic. Good rhythm brings enthusiasm. Stand, close your eyes and feel your feet settle comfortably into the floor. Let the soles open and relax. Bring attention to your breathing. Feel it come and go as the rhythm seeps into you. Now, without moving you feet from this spot, let the music begin to carry your motion. Let it move you. Any movement is fine as long as the feet stay in one spot. As you continue, the pulse and breath directing your movement, let the feet open down into the ground. Feel them. With your inward-facing gaze, observe yourself as you move. Continue for a while. Then, relax your focus and let your body move however it feels for a while longer.
Afterward, lie down and rest.

Unfettered Feet Meditation
Feet are not just for standing and walking. Yes, our legs could just push inert blocks around, but what if instead even a stiff foot wasn't cement? What if it was a hoof with a horny case, a huge toenail? That bit of poetry makes all the difference

Unfettered Feet Meditation
Meditation: Use gentle, undemanding music or silence for this. Lie on your side on a comfortably padded floor or a bed in Low Space. Support your head with a pillow. You may also want a small pillow or soft folded blanket between your knees. Close your eyes and find your breathing. When you are ready,

draw your attention to your feet and let them do any small gentle motions, feeling the surfaces, the toes like tiny anttennae, and the ankles angling and hinging incrementally. The legs mostly rest but if the feet want to wander a bit, let the legs lengthen or bend as needed. In a while, turn to your other side and continue the exploration.

A foot touching the ground is a way of seeing. As feet open they'll perceive the dark air holding no light or sunny warmth, night air empty of vision yet full of whispers, echoes, rustling. Released from servitude, feet go hunting for their myths and dreams. Footsoles open their gaze. What color are their eyes? Toes are like eyelashes or cilia creeping over the rug.

Arches refusing to see, seen too much.
In the middle of night, my feet turn into talons.
— Dunya, Journal Entry

Hands and Feet

Because we typically have awareness in our hands while feet go unnoticed, attending to feet and hands simultaneously stimulates awakening. Often our feet imitate our hands or by being given permission to move freely in tandem, are influenced into greater articulation. The relationship between feet and hands more closely resembles early primate evolutionary stages.

Crossing Center Meditation

Crossing Center Meditation connects different body regions across two different center axis lines.

Crossing Center Meditation

Meditation: Standing, using any moderate delicious music, draw your focus to your hands and feet. Stand on both feet but put 70% of your weight on one foot; the other foot with 30% of your weight now has more freedom of motion. Once you have established this stance and awareness, let both hands and the 30% foot move in their own way, feeling the connection between these distal points. This initiates a diagonal motion crossing your body's centerline. After a while, keep the hands going and shift your weight to the other foot, continuing the movement meditation with the other diagonal motion crossing centerline. Continue for a while, feeling this stance and connection. This time, do the opposite: simultaneously move one hand and both feet, shifting weight as needed. As you continue, take a moment to note the difference between this and the previous exploration. In a while, relax the first hand and let the other hand take over while continuing to move both feet.

After, relax your attention and let your body move however it feels.
After a while, lie down and rest.

In Crossing Center Meditation we explore across two of our body's centerlines—the vertical axis most easily perceived as the up-and-down line of our spine when we stand, and the horizontal axis at our waist dividing us into top and bottom. To discover these we will be moving in High Space, that is, standing upright on our feet. In Crossing Center Meditation, one half of the body, either upper or lower, acts bilaterally— that is, equally on both sides of our vertical central axis—while the other half is unilateral. We receive the stability of the former and the awakening of the latter. What is significant in this meditation is that we are also focusing across the horizontal axis. This evokes a less common movement experience thus opening potentials as well as prodding vestigial embodiments of ancestral function.

Arm Meditations

We spend all our life moving our arms fully in a wide variety of tasks and motions. They are easy to access. You can move them standing, sitting, or lying down. The following meditations each bring us to a more specific awareness within our arms.

Arm Meditations: Ways to Open Your Arms
Close your eyes and move your arms leading with your wrists.
Close your eyes and let your arms move any way they wish keeping your awareness on your wrists.

Close your eyes and let your arms move from your elbows.

Close your eyes and let your arms any way they wish keeping your awareness on your elbows.

Close your eyes and move your arms leading from the back of the forearm.
Close your eyes and move your arms leading with the inside of the forearm.
Close your eyes and let your arms move any way they wish keeping your awareness on your forearms.

Close your eyes and move your arms leading with the upper arm.
Close your eyes and let your arms move any way they wish keeping your awareness on your upper arm.

Close your eyes and move feeling the bones in your arms.
Close your eyes and move the arms and hands being aware of the tips of your fingers
Keep your eyes closed and let your arms move however they wish.

Close your eyes and let your arms move any way they wish to the rhythm in the music.
Close your eyes and let your arms move to the melody line of the music.

Close your eyes and let your arms be large paint brushes painting space.
Close your eyes and let your arms and hands be large tongues, licking space.
Close your eyes and let your arms and hands be large blades slicing space.
Close your eyes closed and let your arms move any way they wish.

In both Arms (and Hips) I offer a simple laundry list of meditations. As in all our meditations, first close your eyes and find your breathing, then settle your attention on a specific spot in your body. Take your time with any of these; they all yield tremendous richness. However, I have also found days when I do several, each for a brief time—just enough to actually feel its sensation—awakening the entire body area fully. Spending time in one spot is deeper and honed in, the other shallower and more comprehensive.

Hip Meditations
As body areas go, there is nothing more potent—or loaded—than our pelvis, so it is odd that I've decided to simply attach a laundry list for you. I think this is because we all know this area will carry enormous potential

for awakening and discovery, and that the slenderest of keys will suffice. Without a doubt your excavation of this body arena will be lush. In my memoir, *Skin of Glass*, I wrote about my three months of daily practice focusing just on ovaries; this topic allowed emotional clearing, but more unexpectedly, aroused mythology and mystery. The laundry list is to keep you company, or prod you on in case you hit doldrums.

Hip Meditations:
Close your eyes, let your hips move, and be aware of your hip sockets.
Close your eyes, let your hips move, and be aware of their outside surfaces.
Close your eyes, let your hips move, and feel the bottoms of your feet.
Close your eyes, let your hips move, and let your legs feel fluid as fabric.
Close your eyes, let your hips move, and be aware of your sacrum.
Keep your eyes closed and let your hips move however they wish.

Close your eyes, let your hips move, and be aware of the viscera in the bony bowl.
Close your eyes, let your hips move, and sense your gonads.
Let your uterus move your hips.
Let your gonads move your hips.
Keep your eyes closed and let your hips be free.

Close your eyes, let your hips move, and keep neck and shoulders loose.

Close your eyes and move your hips in circular motion.
Close your eyes and move your hips in linear motions.
Close your eyes and, using your hips as a paintbrush, draw imaginary lines in space.
Close your eyes and, with your hips, draw your name in space.
Close your eyes and move through space leading with your hips.
Keep your eyes closed and let your hips dream.

Close your eyes and let your hips move to the rhythm of the music.
Close your eyes and do the rhythm with the right hip. Then the left.
Close your eyes and let your hips move with the melody of the music.
Close your eyes and do the melody with the right hip. Then the left.
Close your eyes let your hips vibrate.

Close your eyes and let your hips move any way they feel.
Keep your eyes closed and let your hips dream.

Close your eyes and do the smallest possible movement with your hips.
Close your eyes and do large, gentle movement with the hips.
Close your eyes and do strong, medium-sized movement with the hips.
Close your eyes and be aware of your hips as they do any movement they wish.
Keep your eyes closed and let your hips dream.

Basket and Bowl

How we speak about our bodies influences how we feel about them. Carry, in the basket of ribs, the tender flowers—beating heart, fluttering lungs, and secrets beneath the foot of the tongue. The pelvis as a bowl is a lovely image and gives us a good sense of its job—to carry our soft, oily entrails. The ribs, however, have long been burdened with harsh monikers—rib 'cage' or 'case.' I love the word 'basket' instead. This is airy and light-weight, giving our lungs room to breathe and yet structured enough to protect them. You can feel the basket carrying heart and lungs, best when lying down. The breasts rest on the outside of the basket. The soft tissues come to life as movement rises and sinks through basket and bowl.

Spine Meditations

Attention on the spine's frontal surface takes us within, as opposed to the back surface with its skin-covered pointy protuberances which we can both see and touch with our fingers.

Frontal Spine Meditation

Meditation: Begin sitting, standing, or lying down. Close your eyes. Find your breathing. When you are ready, bring your inner gaze to the inside front surface of your spine, beside where your viscera, lungs, stomach and spleen squish and pulse. Breathing, gazing in, let this frontal surface begin to stir in tiny motions. The motions may be too small to have much sensation. As your inner gaze grows clearer, note where your attention has landed. Is it in the lower cervical vertebrae behind your throat, or thoracic spine in back of your stomach? Once your gaze has settled, let it begin to wander up or down while continuing with gentle tiny motions. If you lose clarity, simply continue to gaze along that area of spine, waiting for it to come clear. Continue with the tiny motions, breathing gently. Take your time.

This time as you continue, let your inner gaze soften, melting into an inner perception, a sense of this area. Take your time. What is there? Void? Creature? Landscape? Dream?

After a while, relax your attention and move freely.

After a while, lie down. Rest.

Being unable to 'see' or perceive our inner structures—the word for this is interoception—may indicate injury or other types of trauma. Tread gently. Be patient, waiting to see if the wounded creature will come out. If it isn't yet time, move on. I like to do this meditation in the morning in bed after that first big wake-up stretch and before I get up. Just a few minutes helps me experience my whole body. It also helps calm me at night when I'm too restless to get to sleep. And—so many uses!—I have used it when I've been too long at the computer and feel the dread freeze take over.

Spinal Breath Meditation

Meditation: This powerful balancing meditation, circulating the body's currents, unblocking held energy is from the Sufi tradition. Begin sitting. Close your eyes. Find your breathing. When you are ready, bring your attention to your breathing and to area behind your navel. Draw your sense of breath here. This isn't anatomical but energetic. Now, on the inhale, gently draw this energy and the sense of breath along the area in front of your spine up into your cranium to the bregma (the crown). On the exhale, the sense of breath and the energy travel back down into the belly. The body is still but not stiff as you do this internal movement of energy. Continue the inner motion of breath and energy.

After a while, relax your attention, and return to your normal breathing. Be at ease as you rest in sitting.

After a while, lie down and rest.

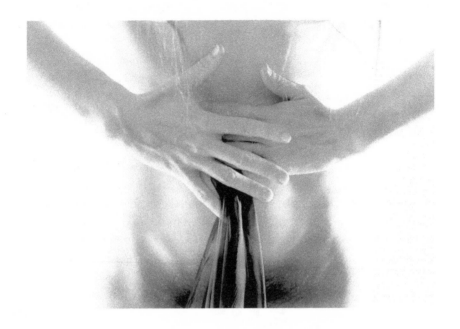

Skin is my mother.
My mother created my skin
out of herself,
then touched it
so I grew conscious of it
as I moved away and away.

Photo by Fritz Penning

Skin

We are so used to living within our skins that we allow them to introduce themselves as neutral envelopes, capable of excitation at the extremities (and at extreme moments), rather than as busy, body-sensing organs. We see our skins as hides hung around our inner life, when, in so many ways, they are the inner life, pushed outside.

— Adam Gopnik, *The New Yorker Magazine* 5/2016

Skin Touch Meditation

Meditation: Either seated or lying down, let the palms of your hands rest on a surface. It can be your thighs or stomach or anywhere on your body, or it can be on the surface supporting you. Find your breathing. Keeping contact with the surface, gently shift your hands to awaken the sensation in your palms. How does the surface feel? Your thigh or belly? The blanket or floor? This time, move with breath awareness, stroking the palms of your hands along the surface. Here is one idea: perhaps, sitting with legs out in front, your hands stroke down over the tops of your thighs, over the tops of your feet, under the soles, then up the sides of your legs as you return. That is one possibility. Move slowly in any direction you like, feeling the surface texture and temperature under you palm's skin.

After a while, continuing to move with your breathing this time drawing your attention to the fingertips, feeling the pads move over surfaces, a very light stroking, the palm hovering, arced or curled above the surface. Continue on. Finally, let your hands move away from surface contact. Let them gently stroke the air.

After a while, relax your attention and let your body move as it wishes.

After another while, let the movement subside. Lie down and rest.

Peaceful and generous, our skin invites us into a sigh of relief. We swiftly flow into deepening. Our palms will warm and grow more sensate as we continue. Focusing on one palm at a time may help hone sensation. The suggested progressions of attention take advantage of this growing sensory feedback as it naturally emerges. Another possibility is to alternately focus on the skin surfaces actively touching—your fingertips or palms, then the skin surface being touched—your thigh, foot, arm, etc. Both skin surfaces deliver sensory feedback. Play with this if you like, though it can be a lot to attend to, and as we head into our deepening, the complexity may be counterproductive. Always remember, the purpose of tuning into sensation is to awaken subtlety, which in turn ushers us beyond ordinary consciousness into an absorbed depth. See how it goes for you.

Four Moments of Skin

One day, when my skin was green and burnt apricot, a flute came into it and shivered it.

Skin is my mother. My mother created my skin out of herself, then touched it so I grew conscious of it as I moved away and away. She traced me, bathed me, drew little socks over my toes, eased my tubby limbs into soft shirts and pants. She wrapped me in my first difference and let me sit to know the new world. All her love is in my skin because she was fascinated by me and my infant skin that has changed but still remembers her. In my skin is my mother.

My skin bristles, opening little baby mouths to the dust and flies and hot desert breath. The mouths unpinch and turn into eyes that blink in bright light and cry when a heart cannot.

Inside my skin, way inside, all is dark and safe. Hidden. Invisible.
— Dunya, journal entry

Skin & Bones Meditation

Meditation: Sitting, standing or lying down, close your eyes and find your breathing. When you are ready, bring awareness to your skin. Feel what it touches—the inside your clothes, the floor, your mat, air. With awareness on skin surface, begin to move in any comfortable manner. Continue with this for a while. You may want to stay on your blanket for the sense of containment and safety; this allows you to deepen.

Now, draw your attention to the movement of your bones inside your muscles. Feel them slide and shift. Let breathing unfold out of the motion's needs. Continue, letting yourself drop down into a deeper quietude. You may lose the focus. This is fine. However, whenever your mind begins to think about anything other than what you are doing, draw yourself back to awareness of your bones. The topic is there to help you; it is there for you to hold onto. After a while, lie down and rest. Let your body sink completely into the ground.

The Primitive Streak and Bilateral Symmetry
What are we before we are body parts?
— Dunya

The Primitive Streak

In our body, what is symmetrical and what is singular? In the very beginning of every body, we are a zygote—an ovum from our mother fertilized by sperm from our father. This potential is as yet undefined. Then our cells do this amazing thing—they process in what is called the Polonaise Movement, a miracle of motion, our first dance. As our cells begin to organize and assemble into basic components, they stream in two directions along rim of the sphere, meet like partners in a formal social dance and troop down the center of the zygote. This forms the Primitive Streak. The Primitive Streak creases the sphere longitudinally in half and will become spine, our centerline, with bilateral symmetry— right and left sides. Two eyes, two ears, two arms, two legs, two lungs, two kidneys. As well, this now-bilateral entity bends a bit at its middle— what will be your waistline—creating cranial and caudal regions, that is, a head and a tail. With the Polonaise Movement into the Primitive Streak, we begin this incarnation's first step to viability. Without it, all further potential is over. This is true for humans as well as sharks, foxes, pigeons, and all other bilateral creatures.

The first Nexus of Mobility Meditation evokes the initiating impulse of our original motion. It isn't necessary to envision the specifics of our cell biology; rather, I have articulated them to show how we are created by way of dance. Now, in motion, we resonate back to this origin. The following meditations are very subtle. They bring this embodied path into true focus. We are not struggling with our minds, observing how our thoughts chimerically create identity. Neither have we any concern for emotion and passion. In this Path we connect to life force itself. Movement reaches deeply in and points toward that which draws us into flesh form so we can undertake the gift and struggle of consciousness.

Nexus of Mobility Meditation

Meditation: Bring your attention to the pelvis and upper thighs, our nexus of mobility. Bring attention to the bony structures—pelvic bowl, lower spine, hip sockets—and the soft tissues—viscera, intestines, reproductive organs, bladder. Bring your attention just here. And then, also bring your attention to your breathing. Though the mechanism of breathing lies above the pelvis, the gentle push-pull of the breath undulates through the bony spine and the soft tissues. As you sit, move ever-so-gently. With attention in the pelvis, let all else melt away. We are with the harder boney tissues, and we are with the viscous tissues, and also the fluid systems, the airy gases, and the energy. The light of our awareness on this arena is the invitation for it to emerge; for it to guide us to its nature; for our self constructions to subside; for the 'what' to overtake the 'who.'

After a while, stand and begin to move. Take your time. Let your attention be light but engaged.

Eventually, complete what you are doing and lie down and rest.

Drawing attention to this seat of our existence brings us our nexus of mobility which gives us agency in this world. This time we invite connection with the original initiative motion from spherical zygote into the folding in. I have found this practice to be so fundamental that it leaps over rationality into the energy out of which cognition and affect are fashioned. This is often the case the farther we regress into our embodiment. Here we are then, in the seat of self, our pelvis and upper thighs, breathing, perceiving the soft inner darkness of squishes and pushes and gurgles, spreading wide, heavy. Our buttocks would mat the spring grass under us. Bring awareness here. I won't say what you will find beneath the stacked chakras. I recently had the most unusual experience coming from this meditation.

I Move

I move. I am on the outside of the motion. My mind clatters off the table. It slips and slides, trying to find a way to stay. The music, the sensation, the visualization. Between and amongst the small efforts, I begin to arrive. My attention on the area of pelvis and upper thighs. I enter into the movement swinging around the joints, stitching through organs. I don't know if I feel what I do or flow beneath sensation. This goes on and on. A small battle with my mind *that attempts to tell me things, or take me away from here. I draw it back again and again. It is confounded, broken into smaller fragments by the music and by an arrow slinging through my belly, fleet and lovely. This goes on and on.*

Sometime later, the music changes. It is the plangent croon of Baaba Maal. He carries the desert in his throat and spills it through me. I have slung my veil over my shoulder. I tramp over the ground, the fur of rug like grass, but also like the backs of lambs that graze in a foreign land. I turn and back away, one hand holding the end of my veil at my navel, the rest of the veil rolled and crumpled, spooling out from me in a long rope along the ground. I see it. My umbilicus.

My umbilicus is the sort of image I would have expected at some point over the years to have conjured, but for some reason never did. Today, up it comes on its own from my pelvis and upper thighs. In these weeks at home during COVID, I have been thinking of my mother. She isn't on Earth; I have been living a long time without her. I miss her more than ever....The veil becoming the umbilical cord connected me once again to her. This is how deep we run. How deep we dance.

— Dunya, journal entry

Light & Shadow Meditation

Meditation: Stand, sit, or lie down. Close your eyes and find your breathing. Now imagine a line down the center of your body. One side of the body is shadowed and the other lit. Take your time gazing inwardly at this. When you are ready, move any way you feel with your attention on the lit side of the body. Feel what is inside skin and fascia. Let it come forward into your awareness as the shadowed side falls farther into invisibility.

After a while, relax your attention and move freely.

When you are ready, bring your attention once more to the centerline and reverse the light and shadow of your inner gaze. Take your time. Let the other side come forward into your awareness.

In a while, relax you attention and move freely.

When you are complete, lie down and rest.

In Light and Shadow Meditation, using the convention of cloaking one body area to be attentive to another, we reach back to in-utero experience. We are not symmetrical, neither by design and certainly not by our the habits of daily life. For instance, are you right handed or left handed? Well, that's huge! The dominant hand will have entirely different capacity and experience than the non-dominant. We may attribute these asymmetries to cultural learning but there is an earlier root as well. In the latter stages of in-utero fetal growth, we are increasingly crowded inside the womb and gradually compress into a small crossed legged packet, our knees folded up to our belly, our arms clasped against our breast with less and less positional change. One leg is over the other and this sets up an spiraling, asymmetrical pattern in our body which we retain throughout life. Beside dominant handed-ness, we may discover other bilateral imbalances. When I close my eyes, for instance, and draw an imaginary line with my consciousness down the centerline of my body, one side is battered and murky, full of repetitive injuries, organ surgery, even a limb paralysis, while the other is content, pleased, fluid, connected. Asymmetry may be a strange sort of destiny, a path within our flesh that produces two different people.

Photo by Paul B. Goode of Anita Theresa

20 IN WITNESS & INNER WITNESS

What is the respectful way to look at other bodies? Surely this is how we view our own body.
— Dunya

In Witness

In Witness Dance Meditation, we will each move while our partner witnesses us, and then exchange roles. For many of us, moving while being observed is a challenge, while for others, the witness role offers surprising learning. Our emotional experiences in Witness Dance Meditation are often an encounter with familial patterns or societal roles. We take time to sit or move with the discomforts and pleasures of each role. Perhaps, with deepening, we move toward the elemental relationship between incarnation and Earth.

Witness Dance Meditation

Meditation: Witness Dance is a straightforward exchange. One person, the Mover, closes their eyes and moves in any comfortable way while the other person, the Witness, observes. After ten minutes (or however long the partners decide to work), exchange roles. As you inhabit each role, relax, turn away from judgment or self-judgement.

Conclude your non-verbal exchange with a verbal antiphon. One person speaks about their experience in both Mover and Witness roles while the other listens. When listening, simply listen and hear without commentary. Then, exchange roles, the other person speaking about their experience in both Mover and Witness roles while the first listens.

After these exchanges, feel free to converse.

Ocular Purdah

A few years ago, I went through a period of being unable to look at videos of professional dancers, which Martha Graham termed 'athletes of God.' My gaze crawled out of my tissues' sensation and dragged a film over my eyeballs. I saw the dancer mistily, pulled back from what my eyes would otherwise seize—a sort of ocular purdah. I knew too well the work that went into perfecting those physiques. Though the dancers intended for me to look, I felt I was invading them. As my eyes turned them into objects, my own body ached. I was bruised inside. I remembered what I had experienced as a professional dancer, honing my body in the service of Art then discovering, rather than appreciation and respect, being torn and pillaged by audience's eyes. Their eyes did what they wanted with me. Certainly I offered myself in this way, but also, as a woman, I was encouraged to offer myself in this way. One thing is certain, and we all know this: our flesh can be bitten and chewed by the gaze of others.

I began to really penetrate this: what is the respectful way to look at other bodies? Our bodies are full of us. Our bodies are us. We all craft our exterior. The eyes of others read our messages. Through encounter we belong to one another. It is through Witness Dance that our eyes can learn to un-grasp. The inevitable objectification which so often is twisted and hardened into oppression can be swept aside as we fold into an intimate tasting of one another beyond our skins. We become real in another's eyes. We are seen. Witness Dancing helped me reclaim a less victimized and more comfortable interpersonal stance.

As the Witness, by way of physical empathy, the Mover's body awakens a witnessing self-encounter. While we observe who they are, we also see who *we* are watching them. Perhaps for a while, somatic empathy tints our perception of the other's body, but the more we observe our own seeing, the more we can pierce through the filter of our own physical resonance. We perceive less of our self and more of the other person. An opportunity arises. The Mover, a figure so like our self, plucks strings in our flesh. Sinking deep into our body's ground, our body begins to see the other's body, not as a 'who' of image, identity, persona, nor the dichotomous self/other, nor oppositional duality/unity. Not even the notion of One—an all too-easy abandonment of embodiment's trial and truth. As our witnessing body gazes, the Mover gives us the experience of incarnation, our living in our dying, our dying in our living, which is not who we are but what we are—a temporary creature.

Witnessing Dying

I watched my father die. I had never seen the shut down at the end. It took me a very long time to perceive what he was doing. Death was happening to him, his body, little by little, unwinding its complex systems, and he had very little agency in its natural progression. Without question his final three months were hard work. Being in a body is an effort, not so much in what we choose to do, but simply in our flesh's unseen management of gravitational pull and metabolism. We may pay attention to ideas and emotions, the luxury layers of the self, but the essentials—heartbeat, respiration, autonomic nervous system—power beneath. That this is unconsciously accomplished by our Central Nervous System doesn't make it less work. When we are young, we never notice. Illness, stillness, and aging bring bits of awareness.

My father was the Mover and I, the Witness, and only later in reflection could I absorb the movement I had witnessed. It made me think of how, as the autumn cold comes, the dominant green chlorophyll dies and reds, yellows, and oranges, hidden yet eclipsed all year long, reveal their brilliance. Unveiling is a central tenet in the mystical journey. As I witnessed the most naked of my father's unveilings, I felt the departure of his body almost as if it was my own. The moments when I could witness without grasping with eyes, or heart, I could accept not only that he was leaving me, but that I will too will leave. Such seeing was a bowing to the magnificence of our massive, uncontrollable corporeality.

Inner Witness

I've spoken about interpersonal witnessing above, but the process of witnessing is intrapersonal as well. When we take witnessing from the interpersonal to intrapersonal, we explore the nature of our consciousness. We go within to observe our experience and inculcate a quieter, simpler, more solid sense of self. Some traditions call this True Self. Others, the ground of self. I like both. Inner Witnessing is an action leading to a capacity to align with one's Inner Witness. For me, the latter feels at times like a different self—certainly a true and more grounded self. A wiser, saner self. A mature, grown-up self. And also a kinder sort of person. That is my Inner Witness. I like to say that Inner Witness resembles a good parent who watches a child, doesn't interfere as the child discovers how to open the box, climb up, find its own legs, its own mind. The parent makes sure the child does't fall off the cliff but otherwise doesn't fuss. The parent bears witness and keeps company. Inner Witness bears witness and keeps us company. To witness ourselves without anxiety or avoidance or grasping or reviling will take some time. It is the very wide arc of our efforts.

Photo by Paul B. Goode of Zahava Griss (aka Z)

21 THE ABSTRACT REALM

In the Abstract Realm, body is a meta-reality.
— Dunya

In the Abstract Realm, lines and curves are the two basic oppositional design elements—although if you talk to a physicist they might argue that curves are made of teensy tiny straight lines. Mathematics aside, for those of living in our bodies the sensation of doing a curving or bending motion is distinctly different from a straight trajectory. Below, curvilinear refers to curving lines of motion, and trajectories to straight lines of motion.

Surrounding Space Curvilinear Meditation
Meditation: Stand or sit comfortably. Close your eyes and find your breathing. When you are ready, let your body begin to gently move with your breathing. In a while, bring your attention to your hands. Let them be wide paintbrushes drawing on the canvas of surrounding space. Stay with this for a while.
Now, hands relaxed, let your upper arms and elbows be the paintbrushes. In a

while, use only your head to inscribe capacious, slow curves and arcs in space. Then hips. Or any other body part that wants to lead.

Once you feel these wide paths are well established, let's add something to them. Much like vines growing on a trellis, let's ornament the wide paths with little curving motions that twine around the large curves. Let your leading body parts transform into calligraphic pens with small nubs to make these more detailed strokes.

Throughout we are moving in the surrounding exterior space.

Internal Space Curvilinear Meditation

Meditation: This time, find your breath. Bring your attention to the world inside inside your spacious body, beneath your skin, around your bones, threading your soft tissue. Feeling within, begin to sense curvilinear motion in this interior topography. Longer curves travel across planes from one body area to another, possibly passing out of your skin at one spot and in through another (for instance, out through one ankle and in through the other) without leaving the curving path. You'll feel a lot of articulation in your joints. When you are ready, as in the previous meditation, let smaller, more complex curves emerge. Observe how your interior structures influence these furbelows. Take your time. There is a lot of magic here.

When you feel complete, let your body move however it wishes.

After a while, lie down. Rest.

Curvilinear Meditation and the Infinity it Invites

For me, curvilinearity itself is such an important topic it could very nearly comprise a lifelong movement Path. In this book, we have explored it in the Imaginal Realm when we engaged the image of the Vine. In our more somatic meditations, we moved the truth of our curved physical construction. When we move in curving lines, we resonate with the substrate of our human design. Even the straightest of our bones—the femur (thigh bone), for instance—is a slightly torquing column with globular crowns and base. Inside, its cells nestle in the arced walls and cylindrical corridors. A femur isn't straight. Our chunky vertebrae snake up and down in a sequences of waves. Slender phalanges fan out in an arch from the ball-like calcanius (heel bone); a bowl of pelvis, a basket of rubs, an inverted cup of cranium. All curves and roundnesses. Once we journey from muscles and tendons, ligaments and organs into our interstitium, we are an intertwining infinity of curvaceousness.

In the Abstract Realm, we put aside the vine's green sap and its allusion to Earth, sky, and growth. We put aside images, meaning, symbolism, significance, and story. In the Abstract realm, we feel clear, pure motion in a palpable mesh of forces.

Ornamental Infinity

In my two most influential dance trainings, Western Classical dance (Ballet and Modern Dance) and Middle Eastern dance, I experienced two wonderfully oppositional approaches to the abstract design elements of lines and curves. In Western Classical dance, the dancer's body measures and is measured against the frame of a stage's proscenium arch or the walls, ceiling, and floor of a room. This dance tradition is a moving architecture of clean, geometric lines and curves imposed on surrounding space. Condensing the space from three dimensions into two as in video, this orientation of body contained in a frame is even clearer. In a sense, Western dance forms derive meaning from contextual frame.

Then I encountered Middle Eastern dance. The moving geometry of this dance form is unconcerned with frame. Lines and curves move from one body area to another *inside* the body, drawing a viewer's eye away from the surrounding space. As well, the dance's abstract geometry centers on complex ornamentation. In the West, ornament is decorative; in the East, ornament is substance. A single curl has no density, but as curves repeat and split, swooping, looping, entwining through different planes in varying magnitudes, they dissolve any underlying frame, hypnotizing us away from edges and toward an infinite centrality. Which is the point.

In my book, *Skin of Glass,* I wrote about design motifs which are less representative than symbol, allegory, or story. A motif may derive a vine or river, but rather then remaining mimetically bound to that object, it takes flight into abstraction.

Calligraphy

It is widely understood that, though the Koran does not expressly forbid figurative representation, the Muslim artist pulls away from depiction of figures or objects...The artist's endeavors, rather than allegorical or symbolic, become centered on the semi-abstract or abstract in the form of vegetal and geometric

ornamentation. These designs initiate contemplation. What is being evoked?
Barbara Brend, lecturer at the British Museum, says, "...the vegetal ornament
speaks of Paradise [of gardens] and the geometric of order, but it would probably be
more true to say that each is capable of evoking a nexus of thoughts surrounding
those concepts." More importantly, the designs induce a trance state arising from
the characteristic Islamic/Sufic premise that mind and heart are a unified organ.
The role of Islamic art is, essentially, an entrainment. Art invites the viewer into a
shared apperception of transcendent mystery.

Filigree

Perched on one hip, I leaned forward in a wrap of Spinal Twist, one leg crossed
over the other, my linked arms looped through the legs in a Celtic knot. My head
drooped forward from a slender stem of neck like a Bleeding Heart blossom. I
breathed softly into the difficult but satisfying stretch. My shoulders strained
pleasantly, upper arms, wrists, buttocks and back working, tugging within
constraints; the ribs darted sideways in scrimshawed wings from the jewel string
spine. My closed eyes saw pure intertwined bones, unadorned by layers of soft
tissue that would ordinarily fold and tuck into empty spaces like too many clothes
on a shelf; this fleshless body felt loose. The osseous lace brought to mind ornate
window screens in Arabic houses and mosques, a structure through which light
streams. This permeable barrier, which separates but allows a covert view, becomes
an object of attention, distracting the eye from that which it protectively obscures.
Breezes pass through, as well as breath, music, voices, perfume, and strands of
light.

In Islamic art, the universal flowering vine motif imprints everything from
embroidery, bas-relief, ceramic tile, and mosaic to brocade and painting.
Individual filaments clasp one another, dive in and out, marry and proliferate into
a mass that knows no beginning or end. The infinite twining of these repetitive
motifs forms zeman, pattern. It is reversible. The inversion is not only directional;
the foreground and the background alternate positions of prominence as well. This
same reversibility can be applied to time, zemin. Time can move forward or
backward. Zeman, zemin. The oscillation of time and space initiates a rhythmic
interplay, a resonant third entity where the first two elements vibrate ethereally.

Straight Trajectory Meditations

In contrast to curves, our elastic movement is a plaid of straight
trajectories. I leave it to you to find exploratory meditations. You can
easily envision these shooting through. I encourage you to explore that

richness and power. For me, straight trajectories act as a palate cleanser. I often do them to wake from the hypnosis that curves induce and to experience strength and energy and to connect with far distances.

Straight to Center

What is the energy of straight trajectory? It is direct. It does not deviate. I remember long ago reading spiritual advice about following a straight path and immediately assumed a moral understanding concerning external behaviors—the straight and narrow. Then one day years later during a deep meditation, I saw my consciousness turn toward an interior center, and that center opened again and again into an even deeper centrality. It was a concise vision. I understood that the Straight Path lay not up ahead or anywhere outward. It moved toward center.

Some say the heart is the center. I personally stumble over that notion, though it may work perfectly for you. One person's poetry is another person's impediment. I prefer to move straight inward wherever that leads. It is a movement, an infinite heading. One door opens to another. Successive walls dissolve. One vast reality melts to reveal another, each more infinite and subtler than the last. How will you direct your Path? Will you tumble clumsily or gracefully in the turning of its magnetism? It may be a huge mess full of stops and starts as it has been for me, callings accepted then forgotten, illusions smashed into disappointment. However you manage, don't ever worry. Remember, it is a real thing, the most Real thing, a wondrous thing.

> *I thank you, deep power*
> *that works me ever more lightly*
> *in ways I can't make out.*
> *The day's labor grows simple now,*
> *and like a holy face*
> *held in my dark hands.*
> — Rainer Maria Rilke, *Rilke's Book of Hours*

ACKNOWLEDGMENTS

This book would not exist without the wisdom, depth, skill, and generosity of Karleen Koen who not only encouraged me throughout the long writing, keeping me on task, keeping me from flagging, but in the final phase became my editor, a blessing beyond my wildest dreams. To her, my endless and most reverent gratitude.

Thank you, Annie Dean, for test-driving the meditations from the page.

Special thanks to the extraordinary students and practitioners for their openness, sensitivity, bravery, humor, relentlessness, perception, and beauty as we continue to explore this vast interior world together. I am indebted to the many interlocutors among them for important conversations about this Path which helped me write this book. Thank you, Alia Thabit, for honoring and supporting me, and Mary Bond, for confirming my intuitions and teaching me. A multitude of laughing thanks to Laurienne Singer, Celeste Yacoboni, and Karuna Haber for delicious, intense, rich spiritual and artistic discussions. Thank you, Stephanie Rudloe, for design assistance.

Thank you, David Hammond and Jane Schmidt, who kept asking when the book would be finished which really helped me keep going.

Thank you, Ric, for holding the ship steady with loving encouragement.

READING LIST

Gaston Bachelard, *Poetics of Space*

Bonnie Bainbridge-Cohen, *Sensing, Feeling, and Action: The Experiential Anatomy of Body-Mind Centering*

Lisa Feldman Barrett, *How Emotions Are Made: The Secret Life of the Brain*

Sandra Blakeslee and Matthew Blakeslee, *The Body Has a Mind of Its Own: How Body Maps in Your Brain Help You Do (Almost) Anything Better*

Mary Bond, *Your Body Mandala: Posture as a Path to Presence*

Blandine Calais-Germain, *Anatomy of Movement*

Rosemary Feitus, R. Louis Schulze, PhD., *The Endless Web: Fascial Anatomy and Physical Reality*

Thomas W. Myers, *Anatomy Trains: Myofascial Meridians for Manual and Movement Therapists*

Michael Sells, *Early Islamic Mysticism: Sufi, Qur'an, Miraj, Poetic and Theological Writings*

Alia Thabit, *Midnight at the Crossroads: Has belly dance sold its soul?*

Bessel Van Der Kolk, *The Body Keeps the Score: Brain, Mind, and Body in the Healing of Trauma*

ABOUT THE AUTHOR

Dunya Dianne McPherson, choreographer/dancer, Shattari Sufi adept, pioneer in embodied mysticism, and Founder of Dancemeditation™, specializes in opening the wonderment of deep, subtle, embodied self-perception. National Endowment for the Arts Choreography Fellow and NYTimes acclaimed performer, Dunya's academic positions include Princeton University, Swarthmore College, Barnard College, Montclair State University, and New York University as well as Kripalu Center for Yoga, Netherlands Mystik Festival, and SAT Institute. She was featured on the global 2020 Embodiment Conference. Dunya holds a BFA from Juilliard and MA in writing from Leslie University. She is the author of *Skin of Glass: Finding Spirit in the Flesh,* a memoir about dance as a spiritual path, and the guidebook *Sojourn the Inner Heaven: Movement Meditations for Awakening.*

www.dancemeditation.org

CPSIA information can be obtained
at www.ICGtesting.com
Printed in the USA
BVHW072105130122
626141BV00004B/654